Apparition Shrines

Apparition Shrines
Places of Pilgrimage and Prayer

by
Robin Ruggles, Ph.D.

With a Foreword by
Bertrand Buby, SM

auline
BOOKS & MEDIA
Boston

Library of Congress Cataloging-in-Publication Data

Ruggles, Robin.
   Christian apparition shrines : places of pilgrimage and prayer /
Robin Ruggles ; with a foreword by Bertrand Buby.
    p. cm.
  Includes bibliographical references.
  ISBN 0-8198-4799-2
   1. Christian shrines.   2. Mary, Blessed Virgin, Saint—Apparitions
and miracles.   3. Jesus Christ—Apparitions and miracles.
  I.Title.
  BT650.R78   1999
  232.91'7'09—dc21   99–39742
                                                     CIP

Quotations from Blessed Faustina are taken from *The Diary of Sr. Faustina Kowalska, Divine Mercy in My Soul,* copyright © 1987 Congregation of Marians of the Immaculate Conception, Stockbridge, MA 01263. All world rights reserved; printed with permission.

Cover Photo: Robin Ruggles, Ph.D.
Photo Credits: Robin Ruggles, Ph.D.—all except some from Zeitoun, Cairo,
    Egypt and Akita, Japan
    Dr. Hosny El Lakany—pp. 160, 168
    Pearl Zaki—pp. 159, 162–165
    Institute of the Handmaids of the Eucharist—pp. 171, 173, 177, 181 (top)

Printed and published in the U.S.A. by Pauline Books & Media, 50 Saint Pauls Avenue, Boston, MA 02130-3491.

www.pauline.org

Pauline Books & Media is the publishing house of the Daughters of St. Paul, an international congregation of women religious serving the Church with the communications media.

1 2 3 4 5 6   05 04 03 02 01 00

Contents

Foreword

Before Jesus ascended into heaven, he left his apostles with the mandate to spread God's Word to all peoples (cf. Mt 28:26); all nations were to know and love the Triune God, Father, Son and Holy Spirit. Dr. Robin Ruggles' book shows that the Lord's wish has been carried out through the Church's preaching and through Mary's appearances to God's people.

Dr. Ruggles takes us on a sacred journey to different cities throughout Europe and South America, then to the Near East (Egypt), and even to the Far East (Japan). Through his gift for writing he describes how God's Word has come to fruition in our world through Mary's messages to God's *Anawim*—"God's little ones." Mary has appeared many times under different titles, and always as Mother of God *(Theotókos)*, pointing the way to God through her Son Jesus.

Ruggles' vivid descriptions of different people, places and events that led to Mary's appearances open for us a panorama of truth, beauty and love, made possible only by the faith of God's little ones, the *Anawim.* These blessed people come to life in scenes from their homes, their daily chores, and their struggles to be heard by their Church communities.

In addition to the accounts of the apparitions, Dr. Ruggles acts as a tour guide leading the reader to towns and historical sites in surrounding cities. He describes churches and other landmarks that can attract pilgrims. He even tells the reader how to reach these areas by car, train and plane, approximate times involved, and where to stay.

The author's lively style offers an armchair pilgrimage of prayer that can profoundly affect readers and kindle their devotion to Mary. As one woman has recounted, "I have been devoted to Mary since I was four years old. Never before have I felt the urge to visit places of Mary's appearances. Now that I have read Dr. Ruggles' accounts, I have changed my way of thinking about religious pilgrimages and places of devotion to Mary. I now look forward to the blessing of being able to call myself a pilgrim."

BERTRAND BUBY, SM
International Marian Research Institute
Dayton, Ohio

Preface

I have often been asked what led me to write this book. A number of factors converged that led to my decision. I was baptized an Anglican but as a teenager I left the Church, and for the next thirty years I had absolutely no interest in religion.

Throughout my career, I traveled widely. One day in Manila, the Philippines, fear and anxiety overwhelmed me. I was convinced I would soon die (my father had died young of a heart attack and my brother had already had a heart attack). I feared I would never see my young children grow up. At that terrifying moment in the hotel room, a voice told me to look at the label of my shirt. I was amazed to see the word "Jesus" clearly printed in my shirt collar. Immediately a sense of peace flooded me, leading to a feeling that everything would work out for the best. It did.

I returned to Victoria, Canada and told my wife, Belen Socorro (Spanish for Bethlehem and Hope), I wanted to return to the Church. Because Belen and our children were Catholic, I soon converted and was received into the Catholic Church in May 1987 (the month of Mary in the Marian year being celebrated by the Catholic Church). I felt Our Blessed Mother had touched my life and I wanted to do something in return.

On a trip to Washington, I packed copies of Catherine Odell's *Those Who Saw Her: The Apparitions of Mary* and John Delaney's *A Woman Clothed with the Sun.* It was fascinating reading but I longed to see what these shrines looked like. The more books I read, the more I found that there were no extensively illustrated overviews of the most famous Marian apparition shrines. Only the fortunate few among pilgrims could visit all the major shrines. Others who, for financial or health reasons, could not travel to Europe, Asia and Latin America would have to be armchair pilgrims. This book is intended for them.

I increasingly felt an interior urging which prodded me year after year to design a photo pilgrimage of Our Lady's shrines celebrating her appearances. I felt that Our Lady was inviting me to put together this work. From 1988 to 1998 I visited most of the major apparition shrines at least three times.

It is difficult to say which shrine I prefer. Each one offers something unique to the pilgrim, and all convey serenity, blessed by a touch from the divine. For me, nothing surpasses the majestic surroundings of La Salette, high in the French Alps. The stained glass window of the scarlet cross in the Basilica of Pontmain stands out as the most stunning one I have viewed. The Eucharistic adoration chapel in Fatima and the midnight Masses in Knock, Ireland and Betania, Venezuela etched themselves into my memory. I felt thrilled to view the evidence of Our Lady's appearances in Akita, Japan and Zeitoun, Cairo. The resting place of Jacinta Marto in the Fatima Basilica is particularly moving as one recalls the courageous example of this six-year-old who joyfully accepted the pain of her terminal illness in reparation for the sins of others.

I personally believe that Our Blessed Mother's appearances call us to conversion, to turn away from sin, and to be reconciled with God and others. To do this, we need to consecrate ourselves to the Sacred Heart of Jesus, font of divine mercy, and the Immaculate Heart of Mary. We must practice mercy if we expect to receive it from God. Mary's messages often invite us to prayer. Perhaps Mary's increasing appearances on earth during the 20th century are a special grace to call us to repent and return to God.

Many drafts were prepared for most chapters of this book. I am greatly indebted to my friend and colleague in Colombia, Dr. Thomas Hargrove, who edited the chapters and provided many useful suggestions, always with encouragement and humor. He has dedicated his life to research centers that help poor farmers improve their livelihoods. While driving to work on September 23, 1994, Dr. Hargrove was kidnapped in Cauca, outside Cali, by the FARC *(Fuerzas Armadas Revolucionarias de Colombia)* guerillas. His friends attended special Masses for him and more than one thousand participants joined in a silent march, calling for his release. He was finally released eleven months later and returned to his family before safely leaving Colombia.

I would also like to thank Cali photographers Mauricio Antorveza and Juan Carlos Quintana for their advice in the selection of the photographs for this book.

I am especially indebted to my wife Belen, my son Michael-Andres and my daughter, Jaseleen-Andrea who gave me their unconditional support over the past ten years, even though it meant less time for them. Belen accompanied me to the European and Mexican shrines and encouraged me to continue when unforeseen obstacles occurred, such as the temporary loss of her passport and papers. My daughter nicknamed my guardian angel "Bugatee" and this friendly spirit frequently acknowledged my prayers during my travels by flashing a light in my mind like a ray of lightning.

Most of all, I would like to dedicate this work to Mary, Mother of the Church and all humanity. I thank her for renewing my faith and guiding me on the path to her Son, Our Lord. In 1988 I began visiting the most famous Marian apparition sanctuaries. True to her mediating role, she led me to her Son. I was fortunate in finally having the satisfaction ten years later to complete my work by visiting the beautiful sanctuaries celebrating our Lord's appearance to St. Margaret Mary Alacoque in Paray-le-Monial, France and to Sister Faustina in Krakow, Poland.

Just in time to be included in the book, the Holy See issued a document on shrines. Based on Sacred Scripture, it presents a theology of shrines and can enrich the reader's appreciation of these places of prayer. The document can be found in the appendix.

The accounts of each apparition and its message are based on the various sources listed in the bibliography. If any copyrighted materials have been inadvertently used in this work without proper credit being given, please notify Pauline Books & Media in writing so that future printings of this work may be corrected.

Ottawa, Canada
January 1999

Apparition Sites As Sanctuaries

Shrines or sanctuaries are sites of religious veneration and pilgrimage dedicated to Jesus, Mary or a saint. Some shrines commemorate the actual site where an apparition took place. These holy places are built as sanctuaries of repose to uplift pilgrims and give them new strength. Many pilgrims seek and find blessings through prayer and the intercession of the saints, especially Mary. The messages given through the visionaries urge us toward a life of conversion, penance, fasting and prayer, especially the rosary, as it follows the mysteries of the life of Jesus.

In reading the stories of the various visions recounted in this book, certain principles concerning private revelations need to be kept in mind. In his book *A Still Small Voice,* Fr. Benedict Groeschel, CFR, has treated the topic of apparitions and interested readers will find that book very informative. As private revelations, apparitions do not add anything to the public divine revelation God has entrusted to the Church. Jesus Christ is the fullness of divine revelation. Nothing can surpass what he taught as he walked the dusty roads of Galilee or sat teaching near the Temple. It is important to keep private revelations in perspective.

In this regard, Fr. Groeschel offers an important principle: "No private revelation comes directly from God, and therefore none can be assumed to be inherently true." In other words, a visionary sees an apparition, such as the Blessed Mother weeping as happened at La Salette, or hears words interiorly spoken (a locution), or both. The visionary then tells other people what he or she saw or heard. But in seeing and hearing, visionaries perceive these things through their frame of reference. In reading a message a visionary received, we are reading what the visionary understood and remembered, not the direct words of God or the Blessed Virgin. In remembering and reporting, seers can make mistakes, forget details or misinterpret something. In recalling an apparition, a visionary remembers it in the same way as any other event, which leaves room for forgetting. When the Blessed Mother told Bernadette, "I am the Immaculate Conception," Bernadette kept going over the words in her mind so she would remember them. Honest errors do not necessarily disprove reported visions, but should make us cautious in evaluating them. The apparition of La Salette offers a good example of how a seer's personal experience can influence perception. At La Salette, the Blessed Mother appeared to two children, Maximin and Mélanie, both from troubled families. The children did not at first realize they were seeing the Blessed Mother. Mary said that she could no longer hold back the heavy arm of her Son. Maximin later said he thought her son had beaten her, while Mélanie thought the woman meant her husband wanted to kill her son. As Sandra Zimdars-Swartz notes (*Encountering Mary,* page 31), "Both children were from troubled homes, and it seems safe to conclude that there was a connection between their own family experiences and this encounter with a weeping woman who spoke about restraining her son and about coming chastisements." This doesn't mean the apparition is inauthentic, but that the visionaries interpreted it through the prism of their experience.

Mary of the Immaculate Conception (Lourdes, France)

*Statue of Our Lady in Tears
(La Salette, France)*

That is why the Church does not require belief in any private revelation, which is only a matter of human faith. It is not a matter of the divine or Catholic faith by which we believe what the Church teaches about God's revelation. Even when the Church approves an apparition, no Catholic is obliged to believe in it; it is not a matter of official Church teaching. Church approval simply means that the reported apparition, after suitable investigation, has been found worthy of belief. This approval excludes fraud and deception. But it remains only a prudential judgment on the part of Church authorities, not an infallible decision.

Concerning the messages that are reported, Fr. Groeschel offers another important principle: "A private revelation by definition is personal and therefore must be carefully applied by those for whom it was meant and only within the limits of ordinary human prudence, and never in an unreasonable way or against the teaching of the Church. It must never be considered an infallible guide in any situation." Is the message meant for the visionary alone, or does it have a wider application?

This question is quite important in evaluating messages like those of Fatima or Akita, or others that speak of war or chastisement. These severe, apocalyptic-sounding revelations have to be considered in the wider context of God's merciful love. Scripture teaches us that God is love (cf. 1 Jn 4:8). God does not cause earthquakes or tidal waves or wars to punish sinners. Instead, "He makes his sun rise on the evil and on the good, and sends rain on the

The Virgin of the Golden Heart (Beauraing, Belgium)

righteous and on the unrighteous" (Mt 5:45). Perhaps the messages that sound rather severe can be taken as a warning that sin leads to suffering. Wars break out due to human hatred and sin, not because God causes war. The Blessed Mother could be warning us to repent or to suffer the consequences of sin.

Keeping this in mind, apparitions can be seen as graces from God to help us lead better Christian lives. They can be an important means to lead the faithful to a better understanding of the Gospel. As the U.S. bishops stated in their pastoral letter on Mary, *Behold Your Mother,* "These providential happenings serve as reminders to us of basic Christian themes: prayer, penance and the necessity of the sacraments."

Our Lady of the Miraculous Medal (Paris, France)

The Church Approval Process of Apparitions

Because it is difficult to evaluate apparitions, the Church has developed a rigorous process for investigating them. The local bishop in whose diocese an apparition has occurred has the option of investigating and deciding whether or not it is worthy of belief by the faithful. Official recognition implies that the apparitions are supernatural, because natural law cannot explain them. They reflect a divine presence, a direct sign from Our Lady to repent and return to God.

Usually the local bishop, if convinced of the apparition, will issue a statement that the content of the message is according to the faith and doctrine of the Church. In some cases, (e.g., Betania, Venezuela) the local bishop has taken the additional step indicating that the apparition itself can be considered authentic.

Diocesan commissions have investigated, and local bishops have approved, nine apparitions:

Rue du Bac (Paris, France, 1830)

La Salette (France, 1846)	Beauraing (Belgium, 1932–1933)
Lourdes (France, 1858)	Banneux (Belgium, 1933)
Pontmain (France, 1871)	Akita (Japan, 1973)
Fatima (Portugal, 1917)	Betania (Cua, Venezuela, 1984)

The Roman Catholic Church has unofficially approved two other apparitions as evidenced by papal visits and gifts, centuries later. They are:

Guadalupe (Mexico, 1531)   Knock (Ireland, 1879)

The Bishop of the Coptic Orthodox Church in Cairo, Egypt has recognized a 1968 apparition of the Virgin Mary at a church in Zeitoun.

This book is intended as a pilgrimage to the twelve approved apparition sanctuaries of the Blessed Virgin, and also includes the two most famous shrines where Our Lord Jesus Christ appeared. The first is in Paray-le-Monial, France, where Our Lord appeared to St. Margaret Mary and revealed his Sacred Heart. The second is the church in Krakow, Poland, commemorating Our Lord's appearance to St. Faustina.

The Divine Mercy
(Krakow, Poland)

St. Margaret Mary to whom Jesus
revealed his Sacred Heart
(Paray-le-Monial, France)

These shrines are found in many different settings: on busy streets in Paris and Cairo, high in the French Alps, in rural areas of Japan and Venezuela, in villages of Portugal, Belgium and Ireland, and in the sprawling urban capital of Mexico City. They have one thing in common: a touch by divinity. These sacred places beckon pilgrims, through earthly sojourns, to experience the divine presence.

Miraculous healings have been associated with most of these shrines—healings that defy medical explanation. For Church authorities, the tremendous number of conversions and people returning to the Church and its sacraments have been even more important than the physical healings. While the miraculous cures testify to God's power, they also signify the inner conversion to the Gospel that takes precedence over everything else. When Jesus healed the paralyzed man who was lowered through the roof, the

Lord indicated this was "so that you may know that the Son of Man has authority on earth to forgive sins" (Lk 5:23). Similarly, the miracles obtained through the intercession of Mary and the saints lead to faith in Christ.

Overview of the Apparition Shrines in This Book

Table One indicates the days of celebration and the estimated number of annual pilgrims to each of the shrines reviewed.

You are now invited to journey to the major apparition shrines of the Virgin Mary and Jesus that local bishops and the Catholic Church (and in the case of Zeitoun, the Coptic Church) have endorsed implicitly or explicitly as worthy of belief.

Many of the shrines are set in beautiful locations, with fountains and gardens. They have inspiring paintings, frescoes and stained glass windows that portray scenes of the rosary and the Way of the Cross. An atmosphere of prayer surrounds the churches, grottos and chapels of perpetual adoration. All give the pilgrim a feeling of harmony with God's universe and a renewed strength of faith.

The springs near the shrine of Guadalupe (Mexico)

The Garden of Mary (Akita, Japan)

*Way of the Cross at
the Shrine in Knock, Ireland*

*Painting of the Trinity in the
new basilica of Guadalupe*

Table One

Shrine	Location
Our Lady of Guadalupe	Mexico City, Mexico
The Sacred Heart of Jesus	Paray-le-Monial, France
Our Lady of the Miraculous Medal	Rue du Bac, Paris, France
Our Lady in Tears	La Salette, France
Our Lady of the Immaculate Conception	Lourdes, France
Our Lady of Prayer	Pontmain, France
Our Lady of Silence	Knock, Ireland
Our Lady of the Rosary	Fatima, Portugal
The Merciful Jesus	Krakow, Poland
The Virgin of the Golden Heart	Beauraing, Belgium
The Virgin of the Poor	Banneux, Belgium
Our Lady, Mother of All People	Zeitoun, Egypt
Our Lady of Akita	Akita, Japan
Our Lady, Reconciler of All People and Nations	Betania, Venezuela

CELEBRATION DAYS AND POPULARITY
OF THE MAJOR APPARITION SHRINES

Celebration Date	Annual Number of Pilgrims
December 12	15–20 million
Friday after the Second Sunday after Pentecost	70,000
November 27	1 million
September 19	250,000
February 11	5 million
January 17	350,000
August 21	1 million
October 13	2 million
Sunday after Easter	1 million
August 22	1 million
January 15	500,000
April 2	Not available
October 13	10,000
March 25	100,000

World Map

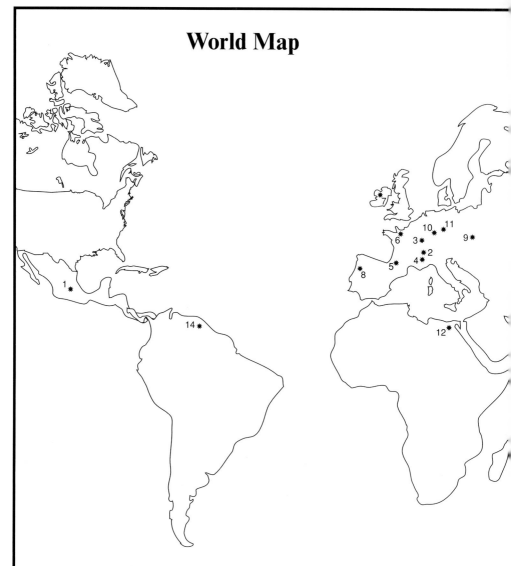

1. Mexico City, Mexico (1531) Our Lady of Guadalupe
2. Paray-le-Monial, France (1673–1675) The Sacred Heart of Jesus
3. Rue du Bac, Paris, France (1830) Our Lady of the Miraculous Medal
4. La Salette, France (1846) Our Lady in Tears
5. Lourdes, France (1858) Our Lady of the Immaculate Conception
6. Pontmain, France (1871) Our Lady of Prayer
7. Knock, Ireland (1879) Our Lady of Silence
8. Fatima, Portugal (1917) Our Lady of the Rosary

LOCATIONS OF MAJOR APPARITION SHRINES

9. Krakow, Poland (1931) The Merciful Jesus
10. Beauraing, Belgium (1932–1933) The Virgin of the Golden Heart
11. Banneux, Belgium (1933) The Virgin of the Poor
12. Zeitoun, Cairo, Egypt (1968) Our Lady, Mother of All People
13. Akita, Japan (1973) Our Lady of Akita
14. Betania, Venezuela (1976–1984) Our Lady, Reconciler of All People and Nations

CHAPTER ONE

Our Lady of Guadalupe

MEXICO CITY, MEXICO (1531)

Statues of Aztecs at the apparition site

Summary

The first major Marian apparition the Catholic Church has recognized occurred in Mexico, only thirty-nine years after Columbus discovered the New World. Four apparitions took place from December 9–12, 1531, on Tepeyac Hill, Mexico City. Juan Diego, an

Juan Diego

Aztec widower, heard strains of celestial music as he approached the hillside. He saw an apparition of the Virgin Mary, who said to him: "I am the perpetual Virgin Mary, Mother of the True God, through whom everything lives."

Mary instructed Juan Diego to tell the bishop of Mexico City her wish that a temple be built where she could offer the people help and protection. The skeptical bishop asked for a sign from heaven. Juan Diego took this message to Our Lady, who told him to climb Tepeyac Hill with an impossible mission—to collect flowers from the frozen soil.

But at the summit, Juan Diego found Castilian roses and carefully brought them back to the Virgin in his tilma or cloak. Our Lady rearranged the flowers. "Return to the bishop," she told Juan Diego, "and open your cloak. A sign from heaven will appear." Juan Diego did so, and as the Castilian roses fell to the floor, all saw an image of Mary on the cloak.

How the image was made remains a mystery. Artists and scientists claim that no human could have painted it. For believers, the image is a miraculous imprinting—an authentic portrait of the Mother of God.

Mary identified with the poor by appearing and speaking to an Aztec peasant in his own language, calling for a place of worship on native soil.

The Historical Context

Mexico had about ten million inhabitants in the early 1500s. Emperor Montezuma II ruled the land of the Aztec Empire from Tenochtitlán, now called Mexico City. The Aztecs, who regarded themselves as the "people of the sun," lived in towns surrounding pyramid-shaped temples built for religious ceremonies. Tepeyac Hill was the site of an Aztec temple for the worship of Tonantzin, their goddess of earth and maize (corn).

In 1519, Captain Hernando Cortés, with four hundred Spaniards reinforced by Indian allies, captured Tenochtitlán and claimed the empire for the Spanish crown. Soldiers razed the temple on Tepeyac Hill, like hundreds of others. Spain sent missionaries to open churches and schools in an effort to convert the natives to Christianity, but in the process the native culture was destroyed.

In 1528, Charles V appointed Prior Juan de Zumárraga, a Franciscan, as the first bishop of the New World in Mexico City. De Zumárraga also reported to the king concerning civil matters. The bishop opposed those Spaniards who committed atrocities against the native people.

The Apparition

Juan Diego, a farmer, owned a house and some land in Tolpetlac, about eight miles north of Tepeyac Hill and now part of northeastern Mexico City. His uncle, Juan Bernardino, lived nearby. Juan Diego often walked with his wife Maria Lucia to the Franciscan monastery in Tlatelolco, a village neighboring old Mexico City, to attend Mass. That church, now called the Church of Santiago (St. James) still stands in Tlatelolco. Maria Lucia died in 1529, and

The Virgin appears to Juan Diego

Juan Diego dedicated himself to helping his uncle and living a devout Christian life. He had converted to Christianity seven years before he saw the Virgin.

Juan Diego, now fifty-seven, walked across the barren hills to Mass in Tlatelolco on the windy morning of Saturday, December 9, 1531. Approaching Tepeyac Hill, he heard incredibly beautiful music. The caroling of birds? An angelic choir? A brilliant white cloud appeared, encircled by a dazzling rainbow. A gentle voice then called him by name in Nahuatl, his native Aztec language.

Painting of Juan Diego with his tilma

At the summit of the hill, a beautiful young woman appeared in front of the mystical cloud. Beaming intense white light, she asked Juan Diego where he was going. "To Tlatelolco, to attend Mass and hear the Gospels explained," he replied.

The young woman then spoke:

> I am the perfect and perpetual Virgin Mary, holy Mother of the True God, through whom everything lives, the Creator and Master of Heaven and Earth.
>
> I wish that in this place my sanctuary be erected so that in it I may make known and give all my love, my compassion and my protection to the people.
>
> I am your merciful Mother, the Mother of all of you who live united in this land, and of all humanity, of all those who love me, of all those who cry to me, of those who seek me, of all those who have confidence in me.
>
> Here I will heed your weeping and sorrow, and will alleviate your suffering. And so that my intentions may be made known, you must go to the house of the bishop of Mexico and tell him that I sent you and I desire to have a sanctuary built here.

Juan Diego agreed to Our Lady's request, descended the rocky slope of Tepeyac, and headed south. After waiting some time at Bishop Juan de Zumárraga's residence in Mexico City, Juan Diego was finally allowed to repeat the Lady's message to the bishop through Juan Gonzalez, an Aztec interpreter. The bishop said he would reflect on the message and told Juan Diego to return later.

Discouraged, Juan Diego went back to Tepeyac Hill where he found the radiant Virgin Mary waiting for him. Our Lady explained that she had many servants who could deliver her message to the bishop, but she had chosen Juan. So the next day, Sunday, Juan Diego returned to the bishop's residence. After waiting several hours, he met with the bishop and asked him to build a new church in honor of the Virgin Mary. "To be convinced, I will need a sign from heaven," the bishop said.

Back at Tepeyac Hill, Juan Diego saw the Virgin Mary again, surrounded by a bright aura. She told him to come back the next day and he would have the sign.

That evening Juan Diego found his uncle gravely ill, possibly from typhoid fever. He stayed with Juan Bernardino on Monday, even though this meant missing his meeting with the Virgin Mary. Juan Bernardino, now close to death, asked his nephew to rush to Tlatelolco for a priest to administer the last sacraments. So Juan Diego set out on Tuesday, December 12.

The Blessed Virgin appearing to Juan Bernardino

On the way, the Virgin Mary descended in a blaze of light before Juan Diego on Tepeyac Hill. "I am hurrying to get a priest to give my uncle the last sacraments," the peasant explained. "I'll attend to your mission afterward."

In a consoling voice, Our Lady told Juan Diego to have trust; his uncle would survive the illness.

"Am I not your Mother and fountain of life who protects you in the folds of my mantle? Do not be troubled about your uncle's illness, for he will not die. He is well already. Do you need anything else?

"Climb Tepeyac Hill, where you will find flowers growing," the Virgin Mary then asked Juan Diego. "Gather the flowers and bring them to me."

He climbed the frozen hill and, amazingly, found Castilian roses blooming, out-of-season, in barren soil that normally bore only cactus and thistles. Frost coated Tepeyac Hill, but dew drops clung to the rose petals. Juan Diego filled his tilma with the flowers and returned.

The roses in bloom at Tepeyac

"The tilma of roses will be a sign," Our Lady told Juan Diego as she rearranged the roses. "Do not unfold the tilma until you are with the bishop." Mary instructed him to again ask the bishop to comply with her wishes to build a sanctuary.

So Juan Diego returned to the capital city on Tuesday for the third time in four days. After much persistence, he finally entered the residence of Bishop de Zumárraga, who was meeting with Don Sebastian Ramírez y Fuenleal, the new governor of Mexico.

Juan Diego described his third meeting with the celestial Lady, then unfolded his tilma. As the Castilian roses fell to the floor, a glowing image of the Mother of Christ appeared on the tilma. The bishop gasped. He knew this sign had come from

Juan Diego unfolding his tilma for the bishop

heaven. Everyone sank to their knees in awe and veneration. The bishop then rose, embraced Juan, and begged his forgiveness for doubting him.

News of the miraculous image spread quickly through Mexico City. The next morning, joyful crowds carried the sacred image to the cathedral. The bishop decided to immediately build a small chapel on Tepeyac Hill to serve the faithful while a larger shrine was being constructed.

When Juan Diego returned to Tolpetlac, his uncle told him about an equally astonishing experience. After Juan Diego had left to get the priest, a beautiful lady visited Juan Bernardino, flooding his room with light and radiating peace and love. The Lady told him of his nephew's mission and of the sacred image imprinted on his tilma.

Our Lady also told Juan Bernardino that she wished to be known as the Virgin Mary of Guadalupe. When told of this title, the bishop marveled. The name "Guadalupe" referred to a famous Marian shrine in Extremadura, a province of Eastern Spain. Columbus had named one of the Antilles islands "Guadalupe." Some scholars think that the Virgin Mary did not speak the Spanish word *Guadalupe,* but rather an Aztec or Nahuatl word that sounded similar. The choice of a name pronounced almost identically in Spanish and Nahuatl was fortunate for both groups.

The Visionary after the Apparition

Bishop de Zumárraga had a small stone chapel built within two weeks of seeing the roses and the image of Our Lady. The bishop put Juan Diego in charge of the new chapel and added a small hermitage. Juan Diego lived there, having turned his property over to his uncle. He devoted the rest of his life to taking care of the shrine and explaining the apparitions to pilgrims.

Juan Bernardino died in 1544, at the age of eighty-four. Four years later, Juan Diego died at age seventy-four. Local history says that the Virgin Mary appeared one last time to console Juan Diego on his deathbed. He is believed to be buried somewhere under the building complex at the base of Tepeyac Hill. Only three days after Juan Diego's death, Bishop de Zumárraga, age seventy-two, also died.

Pope John Paul II beatified Juan Diego on May 6, 1990.

The Virgin appears one last time to Juan Diego as he is dying

The Image on the Tilma

The tilma or poncho that Aztec men wore in those days was woven from a coarse fiber of burlap made from maguey, a cactus plant. Juan Diego's tilma measured sixty-six inches by forty-one inches. Our Lady's image is the size of a human: fifty-six inches high. A shell or conch surrounds the Virgin, radiating golden beams of light. The image shows a young woman of olive complexion with rosy cheeks and long, dark hair. Her eyes look downward, while her delicate hands are clasped in prayer.

Standing on a crescent moon above the head and arms of a tiny cherub, the Virgin Mary wears a rose-colored garment with a gold floral design. A greenish-blue mantle, covered in stars, goes from her head to her feet. A black band indicates she is pregnant. Her face reflects great compassion, and a glow or aura to her body suggests a heavenly presence.

Statue of Juan Diego displaying the tilma and roses before the bishop

The tilma has resisted climate, floods, accidents and sabotage during the past four and a half centuries. For the first one hundred years, it was unprotected and exposed to dust, humidity and smoke and heat from candles. In 1791, nitric acid was accidentally spilled over the tilma as the frame was being cleaned. Miraculously, the image was not damaged. The tilma was later covered with glass and is now framed in solid gold.

Aztec tilmas normally disintegrated in less than twenty years. But the sacred image has withstood more than four centuries remarkably well, despite exposure on a damp wall and being touched by millions of pilgrims.

Several official inquiries have focused on the origin of the tilma and its sacred image. In 1666, artists removed the picture from its glass-covered frame to study the image of coarsely woven maguey cloth seamed vertically down the center. The artists pointed out that even canvas must be stretched and made into a firm surface before painting. The tilma had not been treated, yet the paint had not cracked, nor had the colors faded. The image appears not to have penetrated the threads of the cloth.

*Painting that shows how
the cloth of the tilma was made*

Also impossible to answer was how the painted surface of the tilma remains smooth and pliant, while its reverse side is rough and hard. The artists stated that no human could have painted so well-formed a work on coarse fabric.

The respected portrait artist, Miguel Cabrera, concluded that four types of paint had been used, but could not explain how the paint remained on such an unsuitable material. He also pointed out that the figure of the Virgin is off-center, so that the seam of the cloth does not cross her face.

In the 1950s, two respected Mexican artists, Rivera and Mojica, experimented with different types of paints on cactus cloth. They found that the colors penetrated the cloth and were visible on both sides, unlike Juan Diego's tilma. The artists were convinced that human hands did not paint the tilma.

In 1962, Dr. Charles Wahlig, a New York optometrist, studied the unusual images of several men in Our Lady's eyes. Others had earlier observed that close examination of the portrait enlarged twenty-five times reveals the images of several men, most visible in the Virgin's right eye. Two of these images are thought to be reflections of Juan Diego and Juan Gonzalez, the interpreter, as the Aztec peasant presented his tilma to the bishop. The third reflection is believed to be that of Ramírez y Fuenleal, the new General Administrator of Mexico.

Wahlig demonstrated that the eye reflects images like a mirror. In an experiment, he photographed his daughter's eyes and then enlarged the picture. It clearly showed reflections of the people his daughter was seeing. Wahlig concluded that the tilma's image was indeed miraculous; no artist could paint human images in the eyes of a portrait.

Perhaps the most interesting analysis of the tilma was done in 1979 by Dr. Philip Callahan, a world authority on infra-red radiation and a research biophysicist at the University of Florida. Infrared photography can penetrate the varnish coatings of old paintings and expose original paintings beneath. Together with Dr. Jody Brant Smith of Pensacola State Junior College, Callahan examined the tilma painting through computer enhancement of the infra-red photography. Unlike the Mona Lisa of similar age, no sketch or drawing—not even brushmarks—was found underlying the paint. This adds to the evidence that the image is miraculous. The Florida scientists did find, however, that the moon, the sunburst, the gold edging and the stars were probably added after the original painting, perhaps to conceal damage from the 1629–1634 flood.

The Recognition Process

An important historical account of the Guadalupe apparitions is found in the *Nican Mopohua,* written between 1548–1560 by a Nahuatl scholar Don Antonio Valeriano. A friend of both Juan Diego and the bishop, Valeriano carefully recorded the events he had heard Juan Diego recount. This writing became an important source for later Church investigations. In 1557, the Archbishop of Mexico judged the Guadalupe apparitions as worthy of belief. In 1754, Pope Benedict XIV examined a copy of the sacred image and declared Our Lady of Guadalupe the Principal Patroness and Protectress of Mexico. He authorized a Mass for the feastday on December 12.

Statue of Our Lady on the ascent to Tepeyac Hill

In 1910, Pope Pius X proclaimed Our Lady of Guadalupe as Patroness of Latin America. Pope John XXIII further honored her in 1961 by naming her "Mother of the Americas" from the Arctic to the Antarctic. Pope Paul VI presented a golden rose to the Guadalupe shrine in 1966. Only Lourdes, Fatima and Knock have also received that honor. In 1979 Pope John Paul II visited the Shrine of Guadalupe, the first pontiff to do so.

The Shrine

Bishop de Zumárraga led a procession carrying the sacred image from the cathedral in Mexico City to Tepeyac on December 26, 1531. The tilma held a place of honor in the small chapel the bishop had built there.

The bishop is said to have visited the chapel between 1544 and 1548 to ask Juan Diego to point out the exact site of the fourth apparition. Juan Diego hesitated, trying to recall. A spring of clean, cool water suddenly gushed from the ground nearby. Pilgrims immediately saw this as another sign from the Virgin Mary. The sick claimed to have been cured after drinking or bathing in the spring water.

A larger chapel was opened in 1600. When a flood inundated Mexico City in 1629, the faithful moved the sacred image to the cathedral for protection. It remained there until the waters receded in 1634, and Our Lady of Guadalupe was proclaimed Preserver of Mexico. In 1787, the convent of the Capuchin Sisters was built next to the basilica.

The old basilica

Construction of the old Basilica of Guadalupe began in 1695. Dedicated in 1709, it held five thousand pilgrims. On its stone façade, Juan Diego shows the tilma with its image of the Virgin to Bishop de Zumárraga.

The old basilica, with its twin towers, is one of the most beautiful in Latin America. But large cracks now mar its exterior. Mexico City was built on old lakebeds, and the basilica is sinking as the clays compress. It now serves as a museum, with paintings of the apparition. Thousands of plaques for favors received hang on the basilica's inside walls.

Among the memorials at the shrine is a mast from the ship *San Lucas*. In 1565 the vessel sailed into a storm that destroyed all the ship's masts but one. The sailors prayed to Our Lady of Guadalupe for help and were saved. They later brought the original mast to the shrine as a memorial, and a concrete mast has now replaced it.

The mast of San Lucas

In 1911, a church was built at the site of Juan Bernardino's home in Tolpetlac. Above the altar, a painting by Luis Toral depicts Bernardino's miraculous healing.

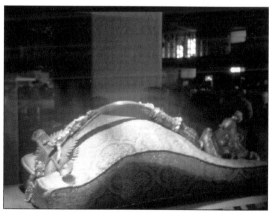

A terrorist planted a time bomb in the old basilica during a violent anti-Church era in Mexico in 1921. Placed among altar flowers directly under the Virgin's painting, the bomb exploded during Mass, ripping

The bent crucifix now displayed in the new basilica

chunks of marble and masonry from the sanctuary. The blast bent a heavy bronze crucifix into an almost circular shape, and damaged the altar piece and stained glass windows. But the explosion did not damage the tilma, nor even crack its glass cover. Neither did it injure anyone in the congregation.

The new Basilica of Our Lady of Guadalupe

A new basilica, designed by Pedro Ramírez, was completed in 1976 and holds ten thousand people. Escalators take pilgrims within meters of the sacred image of Mary, protected by bulletproof glass. The new basilica, almost adjacent to the old one, faces the huge plaza where hundreds of thousands of pilgrims gather to visit the shrine on feast days. From the new basilica one can see *El Cerrito,* the chapel built on Tepeyac Hill at the site of the first apparition.

In addition to the old cathedral and the new basilica, the pilgrim could also visit the Chapel of the Well *(El Pocito)* and the Chapel of the Indians, and climb the stairs to Tepeyac Hill to visit the original apparition site.

The world's most visited Marian shrine, Guadalupe receives from fifteen to twenty million pilgrims annually. From three to four million pilgrims participate in the December 12 services.

Other shrines and altars dedicated to Our Lady of Guadalupe have sprung up in Europe (e.g., San Stefano in Italy), Asia (Nagasaki), and North America. The largest Catholic Church in the

*The Plaza of the
Guadalupe Basilica*

*This painting of the Trinity
hangs in the new basilica*

*The miraculous image of Our Lady
of Guadalupe in the basilica*

United States—the National Shrine of the Immaculate Conception in Washington, D.C., dedicated in 1967—has a Guadalupe chapel. The curved mosaic walls of this chapel beautifully represent the pilgrimage of North and South Americans to the apparition scene.

Planning a Pilgrimage

Sprawling Mexico City has about sixteen and a half million people. Traffic is heavy, but the metro system is efficient. Mexico City and nearby towns offer the pilgrim a wealth of historical and cultural sites besides the mystery, beauty and inspiration of Guadalupe.

Church of Santiago where Juan Diego attended Mass

Excellent hotels, restaurants and shopping are found in the *Zona Rosa* (Pink Zone). From there, the pilgrim takes a thirty minute taxi ride to the Guadalupe shrine. It can also be reached by metro. En route, one can visit the Church of Santiago at the *Plaza de las tres Culturas* in Tlatelolco.

The hub of the city, called the Zócalo, is the site of the Metropolitan Cathedral, the largest church in Mexico. Construction of the church began in 1573 and took two centuries to complete. The National Palace, also on the Zócalo, was the official residence of the Spanish viceroys and now has the offices of the President of Mexico. The Legislative Palace is ten blocks east.

Modern versions of native and Spanish dances are performed several times weekly by the Ballet Folklorico in Mexico City's Palace of Fine Arts.

The National Museum of Anthropology in Chapultepac Park is only ten minutes by taxi from the *Zona Rosa*. The park spreads over forty square miles and has eight museums, several international hotels, some lakes and even a zoo.

The pyramids at Teotihuaacan, among the most impressive in the Western Hemisphere, lie thirty-five miles north. The Pyramids of the Sun and Moon are almost two thousand years old.

Taxco, Mexico

Day tours can be arranged to Cuernavaca, less than fifty miles south of Mexico City. At a lower altitude than Mexico City, its climate is said to be Mexico's best. Interesting sites in Cuernavaca include the Palace of Cortés, the Cathedral, and the neighboring Borda Gardens.

The picturesque hillside town of Taxco, a ninety minute drive south of Cuernavaca, is famous for its whitewashed buildings with red tile roofs, and its intricate silver handicrafts. Several paintings by Miguel Cabrera are in Santa Prisca Church, a baroque classic on Taxco's main plaza.

Puebla, a few hours southeast of the capital, has many beautiful museums and churches, including the main Cathedral with its fourteen chapels, and the Santa Monica and Santa Rita convents.

CHAPTER TWO

The Sacred Heart of Jesus

PARAY-LE-MONIAL, FRANCE (1673–1675)

Chapel of the Apparition

Summary

Margaret Mary Alacoque entered the Visitation Order in 1671 in Paray-le-Monial. She later had several visions of Our Lord Jesus displaying his Sacred Heart full of love for all people. Margaret described the Heart of Jesus as a sun and a burning furnace. Her spiritual director, Fr. Claude de la Colombière, helped to popularize devotion to the Sacred Heart of Jesus, which spread rapidly with the help of the Visitation nuns and the Jesuits. Sister Margaret Mary died in 1690 at age forty-three and was canonized in 1920.

The Historical Context

The two centuries before Margaret Mary's birth saw tumultuous times in Europe. In 1517 Martin Luther nailed his ninety-five theses to the church door in Wittenberg, Germany, igniting the Reformation. Religious upheavals soon spread through Europe, and many Catholic countries broke with Rome. The Catholic Church reacted with its own reforms at the Council of Trent.

Francis de Sales was born into this atmosphere of religious conflict in the Savoy region of France in 1567. He would become one of the best known and loved French saints. In Dijon, the capital of Burgundy, he met the widow Jane Frances Fremyot de Chantal, and they co-founded the Order of the Visitation of the Blessed Virgin Mary in 1610. This religious order grew from the first house in Annecy to eighty-seven houses in France, Italy and Switzerland by the time Mother Chantal died in 1641. In 1626 a monastery was founded at Paray-le-Monial in Burgundy, 180 miles southeast of Paris and eighty miles south of Dijon.

Birthplace of St. Margaret Mary (Vérosvres, France)

Shrine at the birthplace of St. Margaret Mary

Margaret Mary (Marguerite-Marie) Alacoque was born on July 22, 1647, in the village of Vérosvres, twenty miles from Paray-le-Monial. She was the fifth of seven children. Her father Claude, a notary who worked for the Lord of Terreau, and her mother Philiberte owned the Lautecour farm.

As a young child, Margaret stayed for some time with her godmother, Madame Fautrières de Corcheval. The godmother's daughter was a nun and Margaret heard people speak of convents and vows. She felt the Holy Spirit stir in her a desire to give herself to God, a desire that would come to fruition years later.

Margaret's father died in 1655, leaving many debts. Margaret's aunt Benedicta Delaroche and her husband Toussaint, the legal managers according to the will, took over the farm to save it from bankruptcy. The demanding Benedicta ill-treated Madame Alacoque and little Margaret. Margaret's younger brothers Chrysostom and James were living with another uncle, Fr. Anthony, in the rectory at Vérosvres. Two older brothers, John and Philibert, had been sent to a Benedictine boarding school.

Margaret studied at the Poor Clare nuns' boarding school in nearby Charolles for two years and made her First Communion there. She had to return home when she fell sick with rheumatic fever, which kept her bedridden for four years. One day, her mother suggested she pray to the Virgin Mary for healing. Margaret did so and within a few weeks she recovered. But as soon as Margaret got better, her aunt Benedicta forced her to scrub floors, wash windows and do the mending.

Margaret's brother John returned to manage the farm after he had completed his studies at the Benedictine Abbey of Cluny. Margaret, now sixteen, told John she wanted to enter a convent. John persuaded her to stay on the farm for a few more years, finish her studies and care for their mother. Their aunt and uncle had left the farm and Margaret felt relieved that her mother would no longer be poorly treated.

Parish church in Vérosvres

Only a year after John returned to Lautecour, he fell ill and died. Then Margaret suffered another tragedy when her brother Philibert, who had taken over the farm after John, also died. Her younger brother James was planning to become a priest so Chrysostom managed the farm. When he married Angelica Aumonier in 1666, Madame Alacoque suggested that nineteen-year-old Margaret also consider marriage. But Margaret wanted to enter religious life.

In 1669, the bishop came to Vérosvres for the first time in twenty years due to the political troubles in the region. Margaret, now twenty-two, was elated that she could now be confirmed and she added Mary to her name. Her mother was still trying to get her to marry. But in 1670, when Pope Clement X declared a special jubilee year, a Franciscan priest came to visit families in the region. He told Chrysostom that he and his mother should not try and stop Margaret Mary from entering a convent. He noted that young people should be left free to follow the vocation God calls them to.

Madame Alacoque relented and told Margaret Mary she could enter the Ursulines, the oldest teaching order in France. But Margaret Mary insisted she would enter the Order of the Visitation of Mary in Paray-le-Monial, a contemplative order dedicated to prayer

St. Margaret Mary

and reparation. In May 1671, twenty-three-year-old Margaret Mary and her brother visited Paray-le-Monial and saw the Visitation Convent for the first time. She spoke with Mother Hersant, the superior, and knew God wanted her there. Margaret Mary had interiorly heard Jesus say, "This is where I want you." On June 20, 1671, Margaret Mary became a postulant, and she took the habit on August 25. The novice mistress, Mother Thouvant, taught Margaret Mary how to meditate, suggesting she think of herself as a blank canvas before God, the supreme artist. Once Mother Thouvant found Margaret Mary in the garden, kneeling in prayer, her face radiant. Margaret Mary said she saw Our Lord on the road to Calvary and he gave her an insight into the meaning of suffering.

In 1672, Mother Mary Frances de Saumaise arrived from Dijon to become the new superior. Concerned about Margaret Mary's reported visions, the superior told her that her profession of vows would be delayed. Mother de Saumaise eventually changed her mind and on November 6, 1672, Sister Margaret Mary professed her vows as a Visitation nun.

In the ten days of retreat in preparation for her profession, Margaret Mary had to look after a donkey and its foal, ensuring they did no damage in the kitchen garden. Margaret Mary later wrote that Jesus kept her company in the hazel tree grove and she gained an insight into the mystery of his passion and death, developing an intense love of the cross.

The Apparition

As Margaret Mary reported more visions of Jesus, Mother de Saumaise told her to write about the graces she had received since arriving at the convent, so some priests could study her case. Since Margaret Mary had only received two years schooling with the Poor Clare nuns in Charolles, she labored slowly at her writing. On December 27, 1673, the feast of St. John the Evangelist, she was found in a dead faint on the floor of the chapel. When recovered, she said the Lord had invited her to rest her head on his breast. She said that Jesus had taken her heart from her body, placed it in his own for a moment, and then returned it to her inflamed.

Convent garden where Jesus appeared to Margaret Mary

Sister Margaret Mary soon experienced another vision of Jesus. She reported seeing the wounded heart of Jesus separated from his body and enthroned in fire and flames. A crown of thorns encircled his heart, with a glowing cross above it. Dazzling rays, transparent as crystal and brighter than the sun, streamed from the heart. Our Lord told Margaret Mary how greatly he loves all people and desires that they love him in return. Jesus promised to give graces to all who honor his Sacred Heart.

Mother de Saumaise showed Margaret Mary's manuscript to two priests, Fr. Francis of the Benedictine Abbey in Paray-le-Monial and Fr. Peter Papon, the superior at the Jesuit college. Both men reassured Mother de Saumaise that it had nothing against faith or morals. They interviewed Sister Margaret Mary in the convent parlor but she felt nervous and had difficulty answering their questions. Afterward, the two priests told Mother de Saumaise that Margaret Mary appeared ill and needed rest and nourishment. They doubted that the Lord had appeared to her.

Then, in 1674, as Margaret Mary knelt alone in the convent chapel adoring the sacred Host in the monstrance, she saw Our Lord dressed in dazzling white. His five wounds shone brightly and heavenly light inflamed his heart. He asked her to receive Holy Communion on the First Friday of every month. He also told her that every Thursday night she would share the anguish he had felt in the Garden of Olives, and she was to keep him company in prayer from eleven o'clock to midnight.

Sister Margaret Mary asked Mother de Saumaise for permission to do what Jesus had requested. The superior re-

Statue of Margaret Mary at the basilica, kneeling in adoration

fused. At that time frequent Communion was unheard of, even in monasteries and convents. Sister Margaret Mary then became ill. Mother de Saumaise visited Margaret Mary in the infirmary and told her that her requests would be granted, as long as she got well and could do her share of work. Margaret Mary prayed for good health and recovered, so she received the permission she had asked. But these special privileges provoked criticism from some of the other sisters.

Margaret Mary needed guidance in handling the situation. She felt the Lord speaking in her heart, telling her that he would send his faithful servant to her, whom she should confide in. In November 1674 Fr. Claude de la Colombière arrived from Lyons to become the new superior at the Jesuit college in Paray-le-Monial. This thirty-four-year-old Jesuit had gained renown as a teacher and preacher in Paris and Lyons. When Margaret heard him speak to the community, she also interiorly heard God's words, "Here is the one I am sending you." Fr. de la Colombière heard the confessions of the sisters and talked to Margaret Mary. But she hesitated to completely confide in him during that first meeting. When she spoke with him again, she related Our Lord's repeated request that she honor his Sacred Heart by making a Holy Hour every Thursday night and receiving Holy Communion on First Fridays.

Grotto at the Basilica Park (Paray-le-Monial)

On June 13, 1675, the feast of Corpus Christi, Margaret Mary told Fr. de la Colombière that the Lord had granted her another vision while she was receiving Holy Communion from the priest. This time she saw Jesus' Sacred Heart aflame with heavenly light and she also saw two other hearts—hers and the Jesuit's. These hearts merged within the consuming fire of the Lord's Sacred Heart. Jesus explained to her that his pure love was uniting these three hearts forever, so as to bring people to know and love the Sacred Heart of Jesus.

On June 16 the Lord again appeared to Sister Margaret Mary while she was in the convent chapel. He told her that she and Fr. de la Colombière were to work to establish a new feast day for the Church, the feast of the Sacred Heart, falling on the Friday after the octave of Corpus Christi. Jesus told her he would bestow special favors upon all those who honor it.

*Statue of St. Margaret Mary
(Vérosvres)*

Fr. de la Colombière had only been in Paray-le-Monial for eighteen months when he was sent to London, England to be the private chaplain to Mary Beatrice d'Este. She was the Italian wife of James, the Duke of York, who was King Charles' younger brother. At the private chapel of the Duchess of York, Fr. de la Colombière had some success in urging his small congregation to practice devotion to the Sacred Heart. But tuberculosis struck him and the English weather aggravated the illness.

Then in 1678, an Anglican clergyman, Titus Oates, alleged a plot was underway to overthrow King Charles the Second and enthrone the Duke of York, who had converted to Catholicism five years earlier. Fr. de la Colombière was arrested that November in his quarters at St. James Palace. While he was in prison, the Duke and Duchess of York managed to get a secret message to King Louis XIV of France, who asked the English for Fr. Claude's release. On December 21 the priest was expelled to France. He went first to Paris but the Jesuits recommended that he go to Lyons, which had better weather. He stopped in Dijon and Paray-le-Monial to break the journey.

When Fr. de la Colombière arrived in Paray-le-Monial after his long absence, he found things had changed. The new superior, Mother Pèronne Rosalie Greyfié, had told Sister Margaret Mary to give up the weekly Holy Hour on Thursday night. The priest spoke to Mother Greyfié on Margaret Mary's behalf, and her situation improved.

Fr. de la Colombière spent the next eighteen months as spiritual director for the boys at the Jesuit college in Lyons. There, he taught the students about devotion to the Sacred Heart. Because his health continued to deteriorate, his superiors sent him back to the milder climate of Paray-le-Monial. He fell ill with a fever and died on February 15, 1682, at the age of forty-one.

The Visionary after the Apparition

When Mother Greyfié's term finished, Mother Mary Christine Melin became the superior. She put Sister Margaret Mary in charge of the novices, to form them as religious and guide their spiritual development. Some of the novices decided to surprise Sister Margaret Mary by making a small altar with an ink sketch of the Sacred Heart, surrounded with candles and flowers. It was the first

Interior of the Convent (Paray-le-Monial)

altar in the world dedicated to the Sacred Heart. A permanent chapel was built and dedicated to the Sacred Heart on September 7, 1688.

The sisters ran a small school for girls ranging in age from ten to fifteen. Mother Melin appointed Sister Margaret Mary as the new Mistress of Pupils in 1687.

In 1688, Mother de Saumaise received a letter from Sister Margaret Mary who told her she had seen another vision of Jesus while praying in the chapel. Jesus promised that those who receive Holy Communion on the First Friday of nine consecutive months will receive the grace of final repentance, and his Sacred Heart will be their refuge at the last moment. This practice is intended to foster frequent Communion and a life lived in closer union with Jesus.

Jesus reveals his Sacred Heart to Margaret Mary

In July of the same year, Sister Margaret Mary reported another vision on the feast of the Visitation. She saw Fr. de la Colombière with Our Lord, the Blessed Virgin Mary, St. Francis de Sales and a host of angels in heaven. Our Lady told her the Visitation Order was entrusted with spreading devotion to the Sacred Heart, and the Jesuits would assist them in this work.

Sister Margaret Mary began a forty-day retreat on July 22, 1690, her forty-third birthday. God made it known to her that she would soon die, and she told the superior this. On October 16 she asked permission to receive the last sacraments and Viaticum. She died on October 17, 1690, at 7:00 P.M. in the company of two novices.

The Recognition Process

Devotion to the Sacred Heart spread gradually. In 1720, the bishop of Marseilles, facing a plague in his city, consecrated his diocese to the Sacred Heart. The bishop of Soissons published in 1729 the life of Margaret Mary. In 1765, Pope Clement XIII introduced the feast at Rome and consented to a request from the bishops of Poland for a liturgy of the Sacred Heart. Pius IX extended the feast to the entire Church in 1856, and in 1899 Leo XIII consecrated humanity to the Sacred Heart. Pope John Paul II visited Paray-le-Monial on October 5, 1986.

Margaret Mary Alacoque was declared Venerable on March 30, 1824, and beatified on September 18, 1864. Pope Benedict XV canonized her on May 13, 1920. Fr. Claude de la Colombière, the great apostle of the Sacred Heart of Jesus, was declared Venerable on January 8, 1880, beatified on June 16, 1929, and canonized on May 31, 1992.

Replica of the saint in Paray-le-Monial

On the hill of Montmartre, overlooking Paris, the first stone of the Sacred Heart Basilica was laid in 1875, following the Franco-Prussian War. The basilica was consecrated on October 16, 1919.

The Shrine

Now more than a thousand years old, Paray-le-Monial began as a small rural parish when Count Lambert of Chalon-sur-Saône founded a monastery there in 971. In 999, the monks of Paray came under the jurisdiction of the Benedictines of Cluny. Under St. Hugh, the abbot of Cluny, a large basilica was built in the Romanesque style. It became a large prosperous monastery in the Middle Ages. Paray-le-Monial is the best remaining example of Cluniac architecture.

Basilica of the Sacred Heart as it faces the Bourbince River

Today Paray-le-Monial has about twelve thousand inhabitants. The Basilica of the Sacred Heart faces the Bourbince River that feeds into the Loire. Constructed from pale stone, it has a bell tower 180 feet high and two other tall towers. At sunset the stone reflects a golden hue.

Margaret Mary's visions of the Sacred Heart took place in the Chapel of the Visitation. A replica of the saint's body lies in a gilded silver shrine. The Visitation nuns are cloistered, but one can talk to them in the parlor behind the bookstore attached to the chapel.

In 1973 Luc Barbier painted the fresco of the second great revelation. It shows Christ with his arms crossed and his five wounds, especially the wound in his heart, radiating the light of love, as Margaret Mary contemplates the apparition. To Jesus' right the painting also depicts Mary, patron of the Visitation Order; St. Paul; the two founders of the Visitation, St. Francis de Sales and St. Jane de Chantal; and Fr. Mateo Crawley-Boevey,

Side altar in the Apparition Chapel

who encouraged the enthrone-
ment of the Sacred Heart in
Christian families. To the left
of Jesus is the Apostle John,
St. Francis of Assisi, St. John
Eudes, St. Claude de la Colombière, and Charles de
Foucauld, the young French
officer who abandoned his
military career to become a
hermit in the Sahara.

Edgar Delvaux sculp-
tured the high altar in the
chapel; the four pillars show
the four evangelists and Jesus
in the middle, breaking bread.
The nuns' choir is to the right
of the main altar.

Park behind the basilica

*Way of the Cross in the
park by the basilica*

Behind the basilica is the *Chambre des Reliques,* a reconstruction of a nun's room in the convent. It has various momentos of Margaret Mary. A three dimensional miniature scene depicts the history of the town and the life of the saint. A serene park setting known as the "Chaplain's Gardens" also lies behind the basilica. There, one can meditate on the Way of the Cross and the scenes depicted in several grottos.

Paray-le-Monial remains an important pilgrimage site and receives many visitors from May to October.

Planning a Pilgrimage

If arriving in Paris, one can take a train from the Gare de Lyon to Paray-le-Monial. France's TGV *(train de grand vitesse)* can make the trip in two hours. It stops in Le Creusot, where buses take passengers from the train station to Paray-le-Monial. The regular train service takes four hours. Passengers get off at Moulins and take a bus to Paray-le-Monial.

Cluny, site of the famous Benedictine Abbey

While in Paray-le-Monial, the pilgrim may wish to rent a car for a day and visit Vérosvres where Margaret Mary was born. Nearby, one can visit Cluny, site of the Benedictine abbey founded in 910 by William the Pious, Duke of Aquitaine. Over a period of two hundred years, Cluny spearheaded a reform movement affecting hundreds of monasteries all over Europe. It reached the height of its glory in the 12th century. Unfortunately, much of the abbey was destroyed during the French Revolution, although the bell tower still stands.

Within a half-hour of Cluny, the pilgrim can visit Taizé, the community founded by Brother Roger in 1940. It attracts thousands of youth, both Catholic and Protestant, from across Europe during the summer months. The music of Taizé has become famous world-wide.

Northeast from Paray-le-Monial in the direction of Dijon is the town of Beaune in the center of the *Côte d'Or,* the famous wine-making area. Construction of the Romanesque Church of Notre Dame began in the 12th century. Gothic elements were added later.

Cathedral of Dijon

It has five 15th century woolen and silk tapestries made in Flanders, illustrating the life of the Virgin Mary.

The capital of Burgundy with 150,000 inhabitants, Dijon has both architectural splendor and a rich cultural life, including a respected university. The TGV train to Paris takes only one hour. The town was once an important site on the spice route and it is still noted for its mustard. Notre Dame, a Gothic church from the 13th century, has fine stained glass windows and a 12th century Black Virgin, venerated as the Protectress of Dijon. The Church of St. Michel with its ornate Renaissance façade was begun in the 15th century and completed in the 17th. Nicolas de Lacour carved the central tympanum on the front façade in 1551.

The Cathedral of St. Benigne, originally Romanesque, was built in the 11th century on the site of a former Benedictine abbey and rebuilt as a Gothic structure in 1280. Benigne was a legendary figure and his supposed tomb became the object of pilgrimage. The bodies of martyrs, abbots, dukes and princes are buried in the crypts.

The *Palais des Ducs* or the Ducal Palace houses the city's art treasures in a wing devoted to the *Musée des Beaux-Arts.* There one can find Flemish and Italian works including some by Rubens, Veronese and Titian.

CHAPTER THREE

Our Lady of the Miraculous Medal

RUE DU BAC, PARIS, FRANCE (1830)

Rue du Bac Chapel

Summary

Rue du Bac, Mary's first visit in the modern age, began a series of Marian apparitions in France. As the country passed through almost a century of revolutionary periods, marred by attacks on the

Church, the Blessed Virgin met with two children at La Salette in 1846, with Bernadette at Lourdes in 1858, and with the villagers of Pontmain in 1871.

A young Daughter of Charity, Catherine Labouré, had a midnight meeting with the Mother of God in 1830. Catherine knelt by Our Lady, rested her hands on her lap, and talked with her for about two hours. Mary gave her the mission of having a medal struck and distributed—a medal that proved so remarkable it quickly became known as the Miraculous Medal.

Sculpture of Mary with Catherine above the convent entrance

The Historical Context

Catherine was born in 1806, following an eventful period of French history. The French Revolution began with the 1789 fall of the Bastille to a Paris mob, and climaxed in the 1793 guillotining of Louis XVI and Marie Antoinette. By 1806, France began to emerge from this anarchy as Napoleon brought more and more of Europe under his control. Catherine's father, Pierre Labouré, had married a school teacher named Louise Madeleine Gontard. Catherine was born Zoé, one of eleven Labouré children, in the small Burgundy village of Fain-les-Moutiers near Dijon. Her birth on May 2 coincided with the ringing of the Angelus bells, the prayer recalling the Angel Gabriel's meeting with Mary.

Zoé's father was a prosperous farmer. Her forty-two-year-old mother, who was deeply religious, died when the girl was nine. The family servant reported afterward that Zoé took the Blessed Virgin's statue from her mother's room and said, "Now, dear Blessed Mother, you will be my mother." Zoé found refuge in the little church in Fain and often prayed there.

In Zoé's first mystical experience, at age eighteen, she dreamed of assisting an old priest at Mass in the Fain church. He beckoned her to follow, but she turned away. "You do well to visit the sick, my child," the priest said. "You flee from me now but one day you will be glad to come to me. God has plans for you. Do not forget it."

Four years later, Zoé was shocked to see a portrait of St. Vincent de Paul in the parlor of the Sisters' House of the *Hospice de la Charité* at Châtillon, a hospice conducted by the Daughters of Charity of St. Vincent de Paul. She recognized him as the old priest in her dream. She then knew God meant her to be a Sister of Charity, the group St. Vincent had founded. Because her father refused to give her permission to enter the convent, Zoé worked in her brother's restaurant in Paris for a year. But she wanted to follow God's call. So at age twenty-three, Zoé entered the Daughters of Charity at Châtillon as a postulant. A few months later she took the name Catherine and entered the novitiate at 140 Rue du Bac in Paris, a community of 150 sisters and novices.

St. Vincent de Paul

The Apparition

"Catherine," a voice called at 11:30 P.M. on July 18, 1830. "Come to the chapel. The Blessed Virgin awaits you." The voice came

Catherine with her guardian angel

from a small child clothed in white, about four or five years old. Catherine thought the child was her guardian angel, to whom she had repeatedly prayed to help her see the Blessed Virgin. Rays of light surrounded the child, whom Catherine followed through the convent's long corridors. The chapel's heavy wooden door opened on its own. Inside, candles lit the chapel, as at Christmas Mass.

The Blessed Virgin sat in a chair on the altar steps near a painting of St. Joseph. Catherine fell to her knees and rested her hands on Mary's lap. They talked for about two hours.

"I am sad," the Blessed Virgin told Catherine, "that people treat the cross with contempt." The king would soon be replaced, Mary predicted, and religious orders in France would be persecuted. The whole world would face sufferings that would peak in forty years.

The Blessed Virgin also told Catherine that she was to carry out an important mission, but gave no details. She said Catherine was to tell no one except her confessor about the meeting and the forthcoming mission.

A week after the apparition, Charles X, the Bourbon king, fled France for England after a failed attempt to restore the throne. The Franco-Prussian war came forty years later in 1871. The Prussians occupied Paris and the French people suffered terribly.

Catherine with Our Blessed Mother

But the Virgin had offered hope for Catherine and France. She said: "Come to the foot of the altar. There, graces will be shed upon all, great and small, who ask for them."

Four months later, on November 27, while meditating with the other sisters in the chapel, Catherine heard the rustling of a silk dress. She saw a beautiful young lady of medium height. The Blessed Virgin, dressed in white, wore a veil and stood on a white globe above a coiled green serpent. Her outstretched hands held a golden globe with a cross, as if offering it to God. She wore on each finger several dazzling rings of brilliant colors. Twelve stars circled the Virgin.

The golden globe represented the world, Mary explained, especially France and its people. The dazzling rays symbolized the graces Mary gives to those who ask. Some gems on the Virgin's fingers did not emit rays—the graces people forget to ask for, she explained.

Catherine saw a frame around the Virgin, inscribed in gold with the words, "O Mary, conceived without sin, pray for us who have recourse to thee."

Mary wished to have a medal cast with this image, an inner voice told Catherine. A large "M" and cross should be on the back of the medal. Underneath were to be the heart of Jesus, crowned with thorns, and the heart of Mary, pierced by a sword. "Those who wear this medal around their neck with confidence will receive great graces," Mary said.

As a sacramental, the Miraculous Medal is meant to help those who wear it grow in holiness. It signifies the graces obtained through the prayer of the Church and expresses the devotion of the faithful. It is not a good luck charm but evokes faith and love, the key elements of prayer. The medal portrays Mary as the Mother of God who offers the world— symbolized by the golden ball—to God. The brilliant rays streaming from the rings on her hands symbolize Mary as the Advocate who intercedes with her Son, asking him to bestow graces. The "M" on the reverse side represents Mary beneath the cross of her Son. The two sacred hearts refer to Our Lady's part in co-operating with the saving work of Jesus. The twelve stars on the medal, Catherine later told her confessor, refer to the Book of Revelation. There, a crown of twelve stars sits on the head of a woman clothed with the sun, with the moon under her feet.

Mary as she appeared to Catherine on November 27, 1830

The Blessed Virgin appeared to Catherine one more time over the next year. After that, Catherine sometimes heard Mary's voice while praying. In one communication, Mary asked Catherine to arrange for a statue to be made portraying her appearance at the Rue du Bac convent.

The arrangements were to be made through Catherine's spiritual advisor, Fr. Aladel. Catherine made him promise never to reveal her identity to anyone, not even her religious superiors. But at first he doubted her and refused to have the medallion cast. Catherine finally told the priest that the Blessed Virgin was becoming impatient. He discussed the matter with Msgr. de Quélen, Archbishop of Paris, who approved the medal and encouraged its production. The first 1,500 medals, made in June 1832, sold out immediately. More than two million Miraculous Medals had been distributed in Paris alone by 1836. Originally called the Medal of the Immaculate Con-

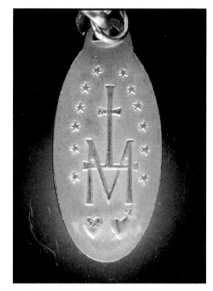

The Miraculous Medal—front (left) and back (right)

ception, it soon became known as the Miraculous Medal because of the wonders worked through it.

The Visionary after the Apparition

Catherine lived in obscurity with her secret for forty-six years after the apparition, caring for the elderly and sick at the Hospice d'Enghien in the Paris suburbs. She avoided the attention that would have come if she was a known visionary.

Catherine's spiritual advisor, however, took no action to make the statue that Mary had requested. In 1876, fearing that she would die and the statue would never be made, Catherine broke her silence of forty-six years. She revealed the secret to her superior, Sister Dufès, who took action to make the statue of the Virgin of the Globe. Catherine finally saw its plaster model, but it took twenty more years before a completed statue stood on the chapel's altar. Catherine died peacefully at age seventy on December 31, 1876.

Miraculous Cures

After Catherine's death in 1876, she was first buried in the chapel basement. A child of twelve, who had been paralyzed since birth, was lowered by ropes into the basement in a scene reminiscent of

Christ's healing of the paralytic at Capernaum. The boy touched the stone of Catherine's tomb and was instantly cured, possibly reflecting God's intention to glorify his servant, Catherine Labouré.

As the popularity of the Miraculous Medal grew in France, so did reports of unexplainable conversions and cures caused by its wearing. One cure was that of a six or seven year old boy who had never walked. His mother gave him a Miraculous Medal and he was healed.

In 1895 the Medal received liturgical approbation—approval for public veneration. The rosary and the brown scapular are other sacramentals that have been so honored.

The Recognition Process

Catherine's body, remarkably well preserved, was exhumed in March 1933. In May 1933, fifty-seven years after her death, Pope Pius XI beatified her. On July 27, 1947, Pope Pius XII canonized Catherine. Her body now lies beneath an altar on the spot where Mary appeared. The statue, whose making caused Catherine so much anguish, stands above the altar. Pope John Paul II made an official visit to the Rue du Bac sanctuary on May 30, 1980.

The incorrupt body of St. Catherine Labouré

The Shrine

The chapel's inconspicuous entrance can be found at 140 Rue du Bac in Paris's seventh *arrondissement* (district). The side street is near the intersection of Boulevards St. Germain and Raspail, and near the Bon Marché, a large department store.

A visit to the peaceful sanctuary, only a few steps from the bustle of Paris, takes one back 160 years. Once past the wooden doors, the pilgrim walks down a long open-air corridor with reliefs of the life of St. Catherine Labouré on one side. The chapel lies at its end.

In 1835 the artist Le Cerf was commissioned to paint the apparition scenes of July 18 and November 27. The two canvasses still hang in the motherhouse.

Entrance to the Chapel

Planning a Pilgrimage

While in Paris, the City of Light, the pilgrim could also visit Notre Dame Cathedral. This beautiful Gothic structure attracts eight million visitors annually. Its construction began in 1163 and took almost two centuries to complete. The stained glass rose window on the west side, completed in 1220, has a diameter of almost

Interior of the Chapel

thirty feet. Its centerpiece shows the Virgin and Child. Notre Dame's gigantic north rose window, with a diameter of forty feet, was completed in 1270 and is the best preserved. It focuses on scenes from the history of Israel. A deep blue predominates and its center shows Mary with the Infant Jesus on her lap. The south rose window depicts scenes from the New Testament.

The three doorways at the front of Notre Dame, built between 1200 and 1230, contain elaborate stone carvings in their arches. The northern doorway and the southern doorway, known as St. Anne's portal, portray scenes in the Virgin's life. The central doorway, known as the Last Judgment, shows Christ seated in judgment of the living and the dead while the Virgin and St. John intercede with him on behalf of humanity.

Notre Dame Cathedral

Inside Notre Dame is an impressive marble scene of the *Pietà* that Nicolus Coustou carved in 1723. It shows the Virgin Mary holding the crucified Christ in her lap. Marble figures of Louis XIII and his son, Louis XIV, are kneeling in the direction of the altar. Six bronze angels surrounding the Pietà carry the instruments of the passion.

The Basilica of the Sacred Heart *(Sacré Coeur)* is found in Montmartre (Hill of Martyrs) overlooking much of Paris. Work began in 1876, after the French defeat in the Franco-Prussian War, and ended in 1919. Its Romanesque-Byzantine style contains a striking mosaic of Christ with a flaming heart, surrounded by the Trinity, St. Michael and St. Joan of Arc.

The Gothic cathedral in Chartres, a town of forty-one thousand less than two hours by train from Paris, has been rebuilt five times after major fires. The church was reconstructed in only thirty years following the disastrous fire of 1194. It was consecrated in 1264 as the Cathedral Church of the Assumption of Our Lady. Its stained glass windows are masterpieces of the 12th and 13th centuries. They were designed to teach the peasants and pilgrims of the Middle Ages, usually illiterate, the principles of the Christian faith.

Three large rose windows depict Christ as the unifying figure. The north window shows Christ as a child with Mary. The west window shows him as judge, and the south window depicts him as the apocalyptic one. Among the 180 stained glass windows (mainly from the 13th century) is the famous Blue Virgin window. Mary, with a halo of luminous blue, is seated on a throne supported by angels, holding Jesus on her knee. The cathedral has more than ten thousand painted or sculptured figures.

Stained glass window in the Cathedral of the Assumption

Chartres became an important pilgrimage site in the Middle Ages partly because Charlemagne's grandson, Charles the Bald, gave the Church the *Sancta Camisa,* which tradition purports Mary wore when she gave birth to Christ. Although not historically verifiable, this relic is kept in the cathedral's treasury.

Louis XIII commissioned Our Lady of Victories Church in 1629, but the church was not completed until 1740. An image from the early 19th century portrays Mary as the Queen of Heaven with the Child Jesus also wearing a crown. In 1836, fewer and fewer parishioners were attending Mass and the parish priest, Fr. des Gennettes, was thinking of resigning. He heard a voice telling him to consecrate his parish to the Most Holy and Immaculate Heart of Mary. He did so and attendance dramatically increased.

Napoleon commissioned the Church of the Madeleine in 1806, and it was completed in 1842. Around the outside of the church stand fifty-two Corinthian columns almost fifty feet high. A marble statue by Marochetti depicts the angels receiving Mary Magdalene in heaven. A giant fresco by Ziegler on the semi-dome of the church ceiling shows Christ encircled by individuals significant in Western Christianity, including Mary Magdalene, the apostles, Emperor Constantine, Joan of Arc and Pope Pius VII. A mosaic of Christ and the saints done by Gilbert-Martin is found underneath the apse.

CHAPTER FOUR

Our Lady in Tears

LA SALETTE, FRANCE (1846)

The Blessed Virgin weeping

Summary

The weeping Virgin Mary appeared to two children, Mélanie Mathieu-Calvat, age fifteen, and Maximin Giraud, eleven, on a clear autumn day in 1846. They were herding cows in a pasture high in the French Alps near the town of La Salette. Sad that many people respected neither Sundays nor the Lord's name, the Virgin Mary asked for prayer and penance. The apparition lasted only half an hour, the shortest one described in this book. Her tears emphasized an urgent call to conversion. The Virgin also revealed some secrets to the children.

The Historical Context

Although the French Revolution and the shorter revolution of 1830 had ended, mid-19th century France still struggled with turmoil. Religion was attacked; fewer people went to Mass, and still fewer respected Sunday as the Lord's day. Widespread hunger had struck other parts of Europe; hundreds of thousands died in the Irish potato famine from 1845 to 1849.

Hard times also faced the families of Mélanie Mathieu-Calvat and Maximin Giraud. They both lived in the isolated mountain village of Corps, but they hardly knew one another. Corps, population one thousand, is fifty miles south of Grenoble along the Napoleonic route leading to the *Côte d'Azur.* The parish of La Salette, in the Diocese of Grenoble, comprised a dozen hamlets, including Ablandins, nine miles northeast of Corps.

Mélanie, one of eight children, begged in the streets until she got a seasonal farm job at age seven. The somber and solitary girl worked for Jean Baptiste Pra and his wife. Mélanie had to take

The children Mélanie and Maximin with Our Lady

their small herd of cows to pastures high in the mountains, stay in Ablandins through the summer, and return to Corps for the winter.

Maximin Giraud also found work in the pastures. For a week, the carefree boy replaced Pierre Selme's herder, who was ill. He seemed happy to leave home for a few days. His mother had died and his stepmother ill-treated him. His asthmatic father drank away much of his earnings.

The Alps at La Salette

The Apparition

The two children first met in the pastures on Thursday, September 17, 1846, then together herded their cows toward the mountain on Saturday, September 19. When the church bell of La Salette rang the Angelus at noon, they lunched on bread and cheese, then lay in the fields to nap. Mélanie awoke in mid-afternoon and began to look for the cows. While in a ravine, she saw a large circle of brilliant light like a globe of fire and called Maximin.

The luminous circle then opened to reveal a seated woman who was weeping, face in hands, elbows resting on her knees. She wore a long white dress and apron, with a luminous crucifix on a

Stained glass window of the La Salette apparition

chain about her neck. On each side of the crucifix were a hammer
and pincers, symbolic instruments of the passion. A crown rested
on her head. A beautiful light emanated from roses of various colors surrounding the crown. A peasant shawl trimmed with roses
covered her shoulders, and she wore slippers covered with pearls.

"Come to me, my children," the woman spoke in French. "Do
not be afraid. I am here to tell you something of the greatest importance.

"If my people will not obey, I shall be compelled to loose my
Son's arm," she told the children, tears on her cheeks. "It is so heavy,
so pressing that I can no longer restrain it…. I have given you six
days for working. The seventh I have reserved for myself. Yet no
one gives it to me. The cart drivers cannot swear without using my
Son's name. These two things make my Son's arm so burdensome
and make its weight so crushing.

"Only a few old women go to Mass in the summer," the Lady
continued. "Everyone else works Sunday, all summer long…. During Lent, they go to the meat market like dogs."

The Lady warned of grain failures and a coming famine. "It is no good to sow wheat, because the insects will eat almost all of what you plant. What comes up will fall into dust when you thresh it. Walnuts will become bad, and grapes will rot. A great famine will come but before the famine, children under seven years old will be seized with trembling and will die in the hands of those who hold them; the others will do penance by the famine." She then whispered a secret to Maximin, and another to Mélanie.

Mary as she wept on the hill

The Lady finished with a sign of hope, telling the children: "If people convert, the rocks will become piles of wheat and the potatoes will sow themselves." When the children did not understand the French word for "potatoes," she switched to the local dialect. She told the children the importance of saying their morning and night prayers. "When time is short, at least say an Our Father or a Hail Mary. Then say more when you have time."

The Lady rose into the air and looked toward heaven as the circle of light around her brightened. Suddenly, she disappeared.

The two children returned to Ablandins. Maximin told the story first, initially to his employer, Selme, then to the Pra family. Mélanie was called in, and she gave the same account as Maximin.

Our Lady standing on the hilltop

Our Lady with Mélanie and Maximin

Mayor Peytard visited the Pra home and questioned Mélanie. Doubtful, he threatened her with jail, but she refused to change her story. The mayor tried to bribe Mélanie with thirty francs, the equivalent of three months salary, to repudiate the story. She refused the bribe, despite her family's poverty.

The elderly parish priest, Fr. Jacques Perrin, put the children in separate rooms and questioned them individually, but he found no inconsistencies. The priest sent the children back to the hill with five adults whose judgment he trusted. The children retold the story to the priest and to the other adults, again with no inconsistencies.

On Monday, September 21, Mélanie returned to the mountain and noticed a spring that had not been there before, at the spot where the lady had appeared. It began to flow regularly, and some miraculous healings were attributed to drinking this spring water.

The Visionaries after the Apparition

After the apparition, Bishop de Bruillard enrolled the two children in a school the Sisters of Providence staffed in Corps to provide the schooling they never had and to shelter them from curiosity seekers. They stayed in the school for only four years.

In 1851, the children agreed to send to the Pope the secrets Mary had revealed to them. In separate locations and before two witnesses, Maximin and Mélanie wrote the secrets each of them had received. Bishop Bruillard read them before sealing the envelopes and sending them to Pope Pius IX. The Pope never publicly disclosed their contents.

Maximin prepared for the priesthood but soon found he was not called to it. He studied medicine, then pharmacy, then mechanics, and even served six months with the Vatican guard. He eventually returned to Corps and died at age forty, on March 1, 1875.

The fountain at La Salette

Mélanie attempted the religious life at convents in Corenc, Vienne and Corps, then later with the Carmelites in Darlington, England, but realized it was not her vocation. She finally found some peace in Altamura, near Naples, Italy where she rented a room and attended Mass daily. Mélanie died at age seventy-two on December 15, 1904, and was buried in Altamura.

Both Maximin and Mélanie remained devoted Catholics. Neither of them ever retracted or changed their stories.

Miraculous Cures

Within a year of the apparition, twenty-three miraculous cures were reported by people who prayed for the intercession of Our Lady of La Salette. Maximin's father was converted and returned to the Church. His asthma disappeared after visiting the apparition site. Furthermore, the local priests reported that hundreds of people began to return to Mass and the sacraments of Reconciliation and the Eucharist.

The Recognition Process

Bishop Philibert de Bruillard of Grenoble began an official Church inquiry by sending four members of the Grenoble seminary to La Salette. The bishop reviewed their report, then appointed two commissions of scholarly priests to examine it independently. The delegates accepted the Virgin Mary's apparition at La Salette as credible.

Statue of Mary at the apparition site

Five years later, on September 19, 1851, Bishop de Bruillard issued a formal declaration authorizing public devotion to Our Lady of La Salette. In this document, read to the congregation at every Mass in the diocese, the bishop stated: "We give judgment that the apparition of the Blessed Virgin to two herders on September 19, 1846...bears in itself all the marks of truth, and the faithful have grounds to believe it indubitable and certain."

The basilica in winter

La Salette soon became a pilgrimage site for people from many countries. On the first anniversary of the children's experience, fifty thousand to sixty thousand people prayed and drank the spring water on the mountain.

The Shrine

On May 25, 1852, Bishop de Bruillard laid the cornerstone of a basilica to be built at the apparition site. The sanctuary, in sienna and gray stone, opened in 1860, although the construction wasn't finished until 1865. Pope Leo

Ceiling fresco in the La Salette Basilica

XIII gave the church the rank of basilica. On August 20–21, 1879, the Cardinal Archbishop of Paris, acting as the Pope's delegate, presided at the crowning of the statue of Our Lady of La Salette and the consecration of the basilica.

A fragment of the stone where the weeping Virgin sat when the children saw her is displayed in the basilica. A beautiful stained glass window above the central doorway depicts the transfiguration. Other stained glass windows show the mysteries of the rosary and the phases of the La Salette apparition. A Carrara marble statue of the crowned Virgin stands in the apse. Behind the basilica, there is a hostelry with bedroom accommodations for 550 and dormitory space for two hundred more.

Painting of Mary's apparition at La Salette

Open for most of the year (but closed in November), the sanctuary and its hostelry are far from the busy world. Snow isolates the sanctuary for most of the winter but it always remains accessible. The majestic panorama of La Salette's peaceful Alpine solitude gives the pilgrim a sense of God's majesty. Its spectacular setting puts this sanctuary symbolically closest to heaven, soaring close to the clouds at 5,800 feet in the Alps.

The Missionaries of Our Lady of La Salette devote themselves as servants of Christ and of the Church to the mystery of reconciliation, in the light of the apparition of Our Lady of La Salette. They have taken the hammer and pincers as their symbol. The hammer represents sin, the cause of the crucifixion. The pincers represents La Salette's charisma of reconciliation, bringing people to experience God's mercy. The sanctuary publishes bi-monthly the *Annales de Notre Dame de la Salette*.

Planning a Pilgrimage

Rapid train service (TGV) enables the pilgrim to reach Grenoble within a few hours of leaving Paris. Daily bus service connects Grenoble to Corps, where the pilgrim can hire a taxi to the sanctuary. In the summer buses run from Grenoble directly to the sanctuary.

From Corps, the pilgrim can drive two hours by car to Laus, near the town of Gap. Mary is said to have appeared to the sixteen-year-old shepherdess Benoîte Rencurel at Laus in 1664.

Grenoble, a university and industrial city that hosted the 1968 Winter Olympics, is the birthplace of the writer Marie Henri Beyle, known as Stendal. While in Grenoble, the pilgrim could visit the Cathedral of Notre Dame, built in the 12th and 13th centuries, and the Church of St. Laurent, a Romanesque structure rebuilt in the 16th and 17th centuries.

From Grenoble, one can journey north to the picturesque lakeside town of Aix-les-Bains whose thermal springs have made it an important health spa since Roman times. Nearby is Annecy, where St. Francis de Sales lived from 1602 until his death.

The pilgrim could also go south to the historic papal city of Avignon, reached easily by train. In the 14th century, Popes lived in the *Palais des Papes,* or Papal Palace, a beautiful example of Gothic architecture with high towers and formidable walls. The Cathedral of Notre Dame des Doms has a gilded weeping Virgin from the 19th century. A 14th century ivory statue of the Virgin Mary stands in the sacristy of the Church of Notre Dame in Villeneuve les Avignon, across the River Rhone from Avignon.

CHAPTER FIVE

Our Lady of the Immaculate Conception

Lourdes, France (1858)

Mosaic of Mary by the entrance to the
Basilica of the Immaculate Conception

Summary

The healing shrine of Lourdes stands out among all Marian apparition sites. There, an impoverished shepherdess, Bernadette

Soubirous, had eighteen visions of the Blessed Virgin. They took place from February 11 to July 16, 1858, twelve years after the apparitions in La Salette. During the ninth apparition, a spring miraculously appeared. In the tenth apparition, the Virgin Mary asked for a chapel to be built and in the sixteenth, she identified herself as the Immaculate Conception. The Virgin's messages helped make the dogma of the Immaculate Conception, proclaimed by Pope Pius IX four years earlier, widely known in France and across Europe.

The Historical Context

Bernadette Soubirous was born on January 7, 1844, in the foothills of the Pyrénées in southwestern France. She fell victim to cholera at age eleven and, although cured, later suffered from asthma and tuberculosis.

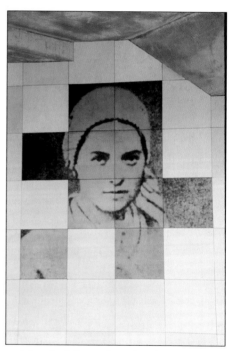

Bernadette lived with her family in a single dark room known as *Le Cachot* (the dungeon). In the back of a workshop, it was a former prison in Lourdes, a town of four thousand inhabitants in the 1850s. Her father, François Soubirous, had lost the family's mill, which had also served as their living quarters. His cousin allowed the Soubirous family to use the small room.

The Apparition

Bernadette, age fourteen, first saw the Mother of God on February 11, 1858, the Thurs-

Mural of Bernadette by the entrance to the Church of St. Bernadette

day before Ash Wednesday. Bernadette, her sister Toinette, and a friend Jeanne Abadie went to search for firewood along the River Gave. At the point where an old canal met the river, there was a

The River Gave by the grotto

rocky grotto or cave called "Massabielle" (the "Old Hump" in the local dialect), where fishermen and shepherds sought shelter in storms.

Toinette and Jeanne gathered wood near the grotto, then left. Alone, Bernadette heard a loud noise like an approaching storm, then saw a rosebush swaying in the wind at the grotto's entrance. A golden cloud emerged from the grotto, and a beautiful young lady appeared above the rosebush. She wore a white veil and a white robe with a blue sash. The folds of her robe partially covered her bare feet, while a shining yellow rose rested on each foot. She held a white rosary in her right hand.

Dropping to her knees, Bernadette took her rosary and began to pray. The Lady said the "Glory Be" with her at the end of each decade. After the prayers, the Lady went back into the cave, and the golden cloud disappeared. Bernadette's sister and friend then returned and, finding her still on her knees, began to ridicule her. Bernadette had been in a state of ecstasy, oblivious to her surroundings.

Back in Lourdes, Toinette told their mother, Louise Castérot, about Bernadette. Jeanne told others. Bernadette's mother forced her to tell the story, then said she had seen illusions and forbade her to go back to the grotto.

But Bernadette returned there repeatedly. On several occasions, the Lady told her in the local dialect to "pray to God for sinners." During the sixth apparition Mary told Bernadette to pray for sinners. A local doctor named Dozous accompanied her on that trip to the grotto. He found her physical condition, even her pulse, normal, although she was in a trancelike state.

Jean-Baptiste Estrade, an excise tax officer, befriended Bernadette and began to document her story. He was there when the

Bernadette meets Our Blessed Mother

village chief of police, M. Jacomet, interrogated Bernadette. Jacomet changed the peasant girl's story, trying to confuse her, but Bernadette consistently corrected him. The police chief then threatened imprisonment if Bernadette returned to the grotto, but she ignored his orders.

The Lady told Bernadette during the apparition on February 25 to drink from the spring and wash in it. This puzzled Bernadette, for the grotto had no spring. She knelt and scratched gravel from the ground where she stood. Water bubbled forth moments later, and she drank it. The trickle of water had grown to a spring the next day, and has flowed continuously ever since.

In subsequent apparitions, the Lady told Bernadette to ask the priests to build a chapel at the grotto, and said that people should visit the chapel in procession.

By March, a crowd of twenty thousand waited along the road each time Bernadette walked to the grotto. On March 25, the feast of the Annunciation, Bernadette asked the beautiful Lady to reveal her identity. "I am the Immaculate Conception," she replied in the Pyrenean dialect. In 1854, Pope Pius IX had proclaimed the doctrine of the Immaculate Conception—namely, that Our Lady was endowed with grace from the moment of her conception and preserved from original sin. But Bernadette did not know what "Immaculate Conception" meant. Indeed, many Catholics in Lourdes were only vaguely aware of the term.

Statue of Our Lady at the grotto

During the apparition on April 7, Bernadette went into ecstasy, holding a candle in her left hand. People gasped in horror as the candle flame licked her right hand while she prayed. But Bernadette felt no pain, and Dr. Dozous was amazed to find that the hand was not burned.

Abbé Peyramale, Bernadette's pastor, initially doubted but soon firmly supported Bernadette and her family. He was won over by Bernadette's report that the Lady was the Immaculate Conception. The priest knew that this poor miller's daughter could not have made up those words.

The Visionary after the Apparition

Bernadette continued to suffer from asthma and tuberculosis for the rest of her short life. She spent her last years as a member of the Sisters of Charity and Christian Instruction at Nevers, six hundred miles north of Lourdes and three hundred miles south of Paris. She publicly spoke of the apparitions only once, when she arrived there in 1865, and was forbidden to mention them publicly again. But, over the years, visiting sisters often asked her questions about the apparitions and she would answer them privately with brief explanations. For years, she received rather harsh treatment from Mother Marie Thérèse Vauzou, who was mistress of novices and later superior. The motive was "to keep Bernadette humble." But some eyewitnesses testified that Bernadette was treated no differently than any other sister.

Bernadette died at age thirty-five on Easter Wednesday, April 16, 1879. Her body, remarkably preserved and visible, lies in a glass reliquary in the convent of St. Gildard in Nevers.

Miraculous Cures

For a cure to be considered miraculous, it first requires a medical examination based on a scientific review of the evidence. Then a canonical investigation must ensure that the cure could not be due to natural causes, but could only have come from God.

The International Medical Association of Lourdes was founded in 1927 to examine the cases of those claiming cures. five thousand physicians from thirty countries and various faiths (Catholics, Jews, Muslims, Buddhists, Protestants) form its mem-

The spring at the grotto

The healing waters of Lourdes

bership and pay annual dues. To safeguard their impartiality, they receive no funding from the Church. To declare a cure to be scientifically inexplicable, the doctors independently review the file and must agree that it concerns a grave illness, accurately diagnosed, difficult to cure, and not going into remission when the person visited Lourdes. The cure must be sudden, not due to medical treatment, and not require a period of convalescence. In addition, no relapse can occur as judged by checkups, sometimes years later.

Cures have occurred during the bath in the spring water, during the procession of the Blessed Sacrament and the blessing of the sick, and sometimes even after the pilgrim has returned home. The waters of the spring and baths have been analyzed and found to contain no special elements that would account for the cures. Cures of organic diseases have included cancers disappearing, bones regrowing and congenital dislocations vanishing.

Cures have occurred from the time of the apparitions. Catherine Latapie, the mother of two children, had broken her arm two years before Bernadette's visions. Two fingers on her right hand had since been paralyzed. Catherine immersed her hand in the flowing Lourdes spring water and immediately felt warmth spread through her arm. When she withdrew her hand, she could move her fingers.

Louis Bouriette, a local stonemason, had been blind in his right eye for over twenty years, as a result of a mine explosion. He put some mud and water from the spring to his bad eye and prayed to Our Lady, and he was cured immediately.

Among the most famous Lourdes cures of the 20th century are the following:

Francis Pascal, a four-year-old boy from Beaucaire, close to Avignon, suffered paralysis and complete blindness following infectious meningitis. He was cured on August 31, 1938.

Gabrielle Clauzel from Oran, Algeria, suffered rheumatic spondylitis or inflammation of the spinal vertebrae. She was cured on August 15, 1943.

The Lourdes shrine

Guy Leydet, a five-year-old quadriplegic, suffered infantile encephalopathy with loss of mental faculties. He was cured on October 6, 1946.

Gerard Baillie, an eight-year-old boy, lost his sight after an operation and was cured on September 27, 1947.

Jeanne Fretel, from Sougeal near Rennes, had thirteen operations and suffered from tuberculous peritonitis. She was cured on October 8, 1948.

Sculpture of Mary giving the rosary to St. Dominic

Colonel Paul Pellegrin, a war veteran from Toulon, suffered chronic fistula resulting from an abscess of the liver. He was cured on October 3, 1950.

Delizia Cirolli, an eleven-year-old, was cured of a cancerous tumor in 1976. The Church declared this a miraculous cure in 1989.

Out of the thousands of cases submitted, the Medical Commission for Lourdes has fully documented sixty-four cures that cannot be explained medically. The Church has declared them miraculous. Seven cures date from 1862, thirty-three from 1907 to 1914, and twenty-four from 1946 to 1978. Ruth Cranston has described many of these cures in *The Miracle of Lourdes.*

Archangels welcome the pilgrim to Lourdes

The Recognition Process

The bishop of Tarbes appointed a commission on July 28, 1858, to study the events at the grotto. After four years of investigation, Bishop Laurence approved the credibility of the apparitions in a decree issued on January 18, 1862. Devotion to Our Lady of Lourdes was authorized and Pope Leo XIII instituted the feast on February 11 commemorating the apparitions. Pope Pius X signed a decree on August 13, 1913, giving Bernadette the title of Venerable. Pius XI beatified Bernadette on June 14, 1925, and on December 8, 1933, he canonized her at St. Peter's in Rome.

The Assumption stained glass in St. Pius X Basilica

Pope John Paul II made a pilgrimage to Lourdes on August 15, 1983, the feast of the Assumption of Our Lady into heaven.

The Shrine

In 1861 the bishop acquired from the town the land around Massabielle, and on October 14, 1862, ground was broken for the future chapel. Bernadette's father worked on the construction. The De Lacour family commissioned Joseph Fabisch, a professor of sculpture at the School of Fine Arts in Lyons, to make a white Carrara marble statue of the Blessed Virgin.

This was placed where the Lady had stood at the grotto. A crowd of twenty thousand, including Bishop Laurence, watched the unveiling of the statue on April 4. The base of the statue bears Our Lady's title, *Que soy era Immaculada Councepciou,* in the local dialect.

In 1884, the Association of the Hospitallers of Our Lady of Lourdes was established to provide nursing and policing services for the huge crowds that came on pilgrimage. The men who serve as stretcher bearers are called *brancardiers.* They come from all walks

Church of St. Bernadette

of life and volunteer their services to help the sick during the peak pilgrimage season, often working long hours.

Crossing the Esplanade to reach the basilicas, one is greeted by statues of the archangels Michael, Gabriel and Raphael. Today, the pilgrim can visit several places of worship at the Lourdes sanctuary, including the Basilica of the Immaculate Conception, the Basilica of the Rosary, the Basilica of St. Pius X, the Crypt, and St. Bernadette Church.

Work on the Basilica of the Immaculate Conception began in 1866. It opened for worship in 1871 and was consecrated on July 2, 1876. In Gothic style, the basilica has twenty-one altars with a statue of the Madonna of Lourdes at the main one. The basilica's sanctuary, directly over the grotto, holds two thousand pilgrims.

The Crypt has five chapels; the central chapel is dedicated to the Virgin Mary. Construction of the Crypt began in 1863, and it opened for worship on May 19, 1866. Perpetual adoration of the Blessed Sacrament is held in the Crypt.

Beautiful mosaics depicting the fifteen mysteries of the rosary give a special solemnity to the Basilica of the Rosary, opened in 1889 and consecrated in 1901. A statue of the Madonna giving the holy rosary to St. Dominic stands over the main portal.

The modern underground Basilica of St. Pius X, consecrated on March 25, 1958, holds twenty-five thousand pilgrims. Behind the throne is the Chapel of the Blessed Sacrament, called *Pax Christi.* This basilica provides for the procession of the Blessed Sacrament and the blessing of the sick to be held indoors during inclement weather.

The Church of St. Bernadette, inaugurated on March 25, 1988, holds five thousand pilgrims.

The Way of the Cross is a path where pilgrims can relive Christ's journey from Pilate's praetorium to the sepulcher. Most of the figures at the stations

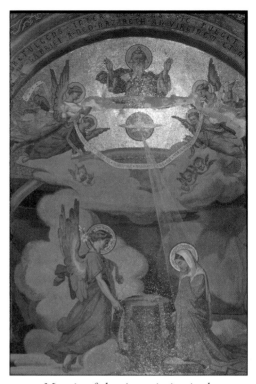

Mosaic of the Anunciation in the Basilica of the Rosary

along the path's 4,900 feet are cast of iron and stand almost seven feet high. A large cross and a white figure of Christ stand before

Votive candles at the apparition site

The Roman Bridge in Lourdes

the first station, which depicts the death sentence. From the last station, which depicts the resurrection, the pilgrim can reach two caves that have been transformed into chapels. One cave chapel is dedicated to St. Mary Magdalene and the other, to Our Lady of Sorrows.

Confessions are not usually heard in the basilicas. Pilgrims who wish to receive the sacrament should go to the Chapel of Reconciliation at the end of the Way of the Cross. There, multilingual priests receive penitents all day.

Lourdes has become famous for its spring water. Rich in symbolism, water reminds us of Baptism and the sacrament of Penance, in which God forgives and purifies us. Springs evoke Jesus' words, "Let anyone who thirsts come to me and drink" (Jn 7:37). More than 120,000 liters of water flow from the springs at Lourdes each day. Since 1974, the crystal clear water flowing from the rock of Massabielle has been exposed to view through an illuminated plate-glass cover. The pilgrim can draw water from twenty faucets to the left of the grotto. The springs also feed fourteen baths; eight are for women, and six for men.

As the pilgrim bathes, he or she usually recites a Hail Mary or another invocation to Our Lady. By tradition, immersion in the freezing water lasts less than a minute. The stark walls of the bathhouse hold only a statue of the Blessed Virgin, which faces the bather who descends the steps into the stone pool and invokes her in prayer. Despite all types of diseases being borne by people entering these baths, there has never been a documented case of contagious transfer.

The Lourdes torchlight procession, symbolizing light and faith, dates from 1872, the year of the first National Pilgrimage. It begins at the grotto around 8:30 every evening in midsummer. Pilgrims begin the procession by reciting the rosary, then singing the "Ave Maria." The torchlight procession ends in front of the Basilica of the Rosary where priests bless the crowd

Planning a Pilgrimage

Pilgrims can easily reach Lourdes by train from Bordeaux or Toulouse. It is about a one-hour drive, mostly via expressway, from the coastal resorts of Biarritz and St. Jean-de-Luz.

Today, Lourdes is a bustling town of eighteen thousand people with excellent facilities for receiving pilgrims. Its four hundred hotels can accommodate the twenty thousand pilgrims who come daily to Lourdes during the peak season. Lourdes has a historical Roman bridge, the *Pont Vieux* across the River Gave, built around 56 B.C. when Crassus, Caesar's lieutenant, occupied the area.

Sunset at Biarritz

In Lourdes, the *Musée Grévin* retraces the life of Bernadette in lifesize waxwork statues. The Pyrenean Museum of arts and crafts provides an exhibit of ancient costumes and houses. Lourdes also has a large indoor pool. Outside the town, one can take a cable car to the Beout, a mountain peak of 2,600 feet, and enjoy a splendid view of Lourdes.

From Lourdes, one can easily visit resorts in the Pyrénées. The spa of Argeleès-Gazost has a charming historic quarter and an abbey church that dates back to a Benedictine community of the 10th and 11th centuries.

Bordeaux, the center of the famous Bordeaux wine region, is the capital of Aquitaine with many fine 18th century buildings. The Cathedral of St. André, dating from the 13th and 14th centuries, is almost as large as Notre Dame in Paris. The crypt of another church, St. Seurin, dates from the 11th century.

Toulouse, the main city of the Midi-Pyrénées region, is known as the *Ville Rose,* the Pink City, because of the color of its brick architecture. Toulouse has an important university and is a major site of the French aerospace industry.

Historic churches in Toulouse include the 14th century Notre Dame du Taur, near the *Place du Capitale,* and the Basilica of St. Sernin, one of the largest of all Romanesque edifices, whose construction began in 1080. The 13th century Basilica of Notre Dame de la Daurade has a black Madonna that pilgrims venerate. The Dominican Church of the Jacobins dates from the 13th and 14th centuries.

St. Jean de Luz is an Atlantic seaside resort and fishing port on the Bay of Biscay, near the Spanish border. There the pilgrim could visit the large ornate Church of St. Jean Baptiste, dating from the 14th and 15th centuries.

CHAPTER SIX

Our Lady of Prayer

PONTMAIN, FRANCE (1871)

*Statue of Our Lady in the
apse of the Pontmain Basilica*

Summary

The Blessed Virgin Mary appeared to four children in Pontmain,
western France, as the Prussians were poised to take the nearby

town of Laval during the 1870–1871 Franco-Prussian War. Mary's visit lifted the curtain of the infinite for three hours, showing a loving, caring Mother of God asking us to pray. No one could explain why the Prussians withdrew the next day. The war ended less than two weeks later.

The Virgin who appeared at Pontmain is called "Our Lady of Prayer," a title given by Pope Leo XIII. (Pope Pius IX had originally granted the title "Our Lady of Hope," but another basilica claimed that title.) Our Lady's mission is to bring to the world the saving love of the crucified and risen Jesus. Images of her smiling face offer peace to pilgrims who visit this sanctuary. During her appearance at Pontmain, Our Lady offered the most optimistic of all her messages.

Laval

The Historical Context

France had declared war on Prussia on July 15, 1870. But it soon suffered setbacks, including the surrender of Emperor Napoleon III and eighty-three thousand French troops, following a disastrous defeat at the Battle of Sedan on September 1. By September 19, the siege of Paris began. One of three Prussian armies, under the command of General von Schmidt, reached Le Mans in western France on January 12 and then the outskirts of Laval on January 17, 1871.

Pontmain is only thirty miles north of Laval, between Fougères and Mont St. Michel, near the Normandy border. Its five hundred villagers feared that the Prussians would occupy their town within days. Many of Pontmain's young men, including Auguste, the eldest son of the Barbedette family, were serving in the French army. A week before the apparition, many in Pontmain saw an aurora borealis on the evening of January 11. César Barbedette said it was a sign from heaven.

The Apparition

Twelve-year-old Eugène Barbedette and his brother Joseph, ten, were doing chores in the barn with their father César on January 17, 1871, a cold wintry day. At 6:00 P.M., Eugène walked to the barn door to see if it was snowing. A thin layer of snow already covered the ground. Eugène looked into the sky and saw a quadrant where no stars appeared on this moonless night.

There, Eugène saw a woman about eighteen to twenty years old suspended twenty feet above the house of Augustin Guidecoq, his neighbor. A dark blue dress, covered with gold stars but with no belt, flowed from her neck to her feet. She wore a black veil that hid her hair, a golden crown, and blue slippers tied with gold ribbons. Three large stars framed the Virgin's face. Eugène called his brother Joseph, who also saw her.

The Barbedette's barn

The boys' parents saw nothing, but called Sister Vitaline from the nearby convent school. She saw nothing but suspected it was the Mother of God, and that only the children could see her.

*Stained glass window of
the apparition of Pontmain*

Sister went back to the school, then returned to the barn with two girls. Both Françoise Richer, eleven, and Jeanne Marie Lebossé, nine, saw the beautiful lady immediately. Before they could talk with the Barbedette boys, the two girls described the Blessed Virgin exactly as Eugène and Joseph had. More than fifty people had now gathered in front of the barn, including Abbé Michel Guérin, who had cared for his parish for thirty-five years.

As the children watched, a large blue oval formed around the woman, and a small red cross appeared on her heart. Abbé Guérin saw nothing but soon led his parishioners in reciting the rosary, then the Magnificat. As the prayers began, the children watched the woman grow in size and the stars on her gown multiply.

A white banner about five feet wide and forty feet long began to unroll just below the woman's feet. The Blessed Virgin did not speak, but the following words appeared in gold, about ten inches high on the scroll: "But pray, my children (*Mais priez mes enfants*). God will soon answer your prayers (*Dieu vous exaucera en peu de temps*). My Son allows himself to be moved (*Mon fils se laisse toucher*)." This message consoled the Pontmain families who had prayed that their village be spared the ravages of war.

Mary's face then changed to a sorrowful expression. She now held a blood-red crucifix about twenty-five inches high. The words "Jesus Christ" were engraved in red against a white background at the top of the crucifix. A star then moved inside the frame and lit four candles that surrounded the Virgin's form, two at shoulder level, and two by her knees. The parish priest had also lit four candles while praying every Sunday in church for their men at war.

Statue of Our Lady of Prayer in the esplanade

The cross then disappeared and the Blessed Virgin spread her arms to the people of Pontmain and smiled. Her expression changed to one of joy, and the villagers rejoiced as the children described what they were seeing. A white veil appeared at the Virgin's feet and seemed to be pulled upward, covering her body. She disappeared from the sky around 9:00 P.M. Her only apparition in Pontmain, it lasted three hours.

The next day the villagers learned that the Prussians were withdrawing their troops from neighboring Laval. This was completed by January 22, much to the surprise of the French military chiefs. The German leader, General von Schmidt, had received an unexpected order the night of January 17 that prevented him from taking the town of Laval, a mile from where his troops were based.

The Virgin Mary had interceded and saved Pontmain because of the faith and prayers of its villagers. The war ended with an armistice signed in Paris on January 28, with the French admitting defeat. Germany took the Alsace-Lorraine region, but Pontmain and Western France were spared. The soldiers conscripted from the parish of Pontmain all returned home unharmed.

The Visionaries after the Apparition

The two younger Barbedette boys enrolled in seminaries and studied for the priesthood. Eugène became a diocesan priest, and he died in 1927. Joseph entered the Oblates of Mary Immaculate and died in 1930. Jeanne Marie Lebossé joined the Sisters of the Holy

Family in Bordeaux. She died in 1933. Françoise Richer worked as a teaching assistant and died in 1915.

The Recognition Process

The bishop of the diocese of Laval, Msgr. Wicart, issued a decree on February 2, 1872, authorizing devotion at Pontmain. He announced plans to build a shrine to honor Mary.

*Stained glass window
in the basilica*

The Basilica of Our Lady of Prayer

Interior of the basilica

The Shrine

The Barbedette barn was turned into a small chapel. Construction of the church began in 1872.

Later designated "Our Lady of Prayer," it has two Gothic towers and overlooks the rolling countryside of Pontmain. The Church was consecrated on October 15, 1900, and Pope Pius X subsequently raised it to the rank of a basilica.

Today, some 350,000 pilgrims annually visit the basilica, the barn of the apparition of Mary, the park of the Oblate Fathers, the Calvary of Pardon, and the parish church. The statue of Mary in front of the basilica is located on the site of her appearance. Behind the basilica is the house of the

Crucifix in the basilica

Oblate Fathers. The Sisters of Evron and the Oblate Fathers maintain excellent facilities for pilgrims.

Planning a Pilgrimage

From Paris, the easiest way to reach the tiny town of Pontmain two hundred miles west is by the rapid train (TGV) to Laval. From there, one can rent a car or taxi and drive to nearby Pontmain.

Many medieval buildings still stand in Laval on the Mayenne River. The Romanesque cathedral was enlarged in the 15th century. The Basilica of Notre-Dame d'Avénières dates from the 11th and 12th centuries and has a Romanesque apse. Inside the basilica is a 15th century Pietà.

Village of Pontmain

Rennes, the capital of Brittany, lies just west of Laval. A 16th century Flemish altarpiece in the Cathedral of St. Pierre depicts the Virgin's life. The abbey of Notre Dame, with Romanesque architecture from the 11th century, is also in Rennes.

The monastery and fortress of Mont St. Michel, along the Normandy coast north of Laval, are on a granite knoll that is separated from the mainland during exceptionally high tides. A statue of the Archangel Michael stands high on the tower of the abbey church. The Archangel is said to have appeared in a dream to Aubert, the bishop of Avranches, and requested that an oratory be built. In 706, the first small church was consecrated. A Benedictine abbey was founded in 960, and Gothic buildings were built in the 13th century.

Northeast of Pontmain in Normandy is Lisieux, a town of twenty-seven thousand inhabitants, where St. Thérèse Martin lived in the Carmelite convent from 1890 to 1897. She wrote *Story of a Soul* and is now a Doctor of the Church. She is buried in a 19th century chapel. Construction on the Basilica of St. Thérèse began in 1929, was suspended during the war, and was completed in the 1960s.

Mont St. Michel on the coast of Normandy

CHAPTER SEVEN

Our Lady of Silence

KNOCK, IRELAND (1879)

Painting of the Knock apparition

Summary

The Virgin Mary, St. Joseph and St. John the Evangelist appeared for two hours before a small group of people in Knock, a quiet village in western Ireland, on August 21, 1879. Early that evening, Mary McLoughlin, Margaret Byrne and her sister Mary Byrne saw a celestial light covering the south wall of the church. They then saw three silent, moving figures. Approaching the church, they viewed an altar with a lamb surrounded by angels before a cross. Heavy rain fell as other curious villagers joined the women. Because she did not speak during her appearance, the Virgin at Knock is called "Our Lady of Silence."

The Historical Context

Knock is a small village in County Mayo, western Ireland, between Claremorris, six miles away, and Ballyhaunis. It is near Castlebar and two hours from the coastal towns of Westport and Lechanvy. On a clear day, one can see from Knock the 2,500 foot mountain peak of Croagh Patrick, where St. Patrick prayed and fasted for forty days in 441.

The potato was the basis of agriculture—and life itself—in Ireland during the 1800s. A staple diet of potatoes and milk nurtured the people until the failure of the potato crop caused the disastrous Irish potato famine from 1845 to 1849. Thousands of tenant farmers, unable to pay their rents, were evicted and left destitute, with no hope of employment or food.

Church of the Apparition in Knock

More than one and a half million Irish people died of starvation or diseases such as cholera and typhus. Another million fled to America. Ireland lost about a third of its population of eight million through death and emigration.

In 1879 County Mayo was one of the poorest areas in Ireland. The people suffered from a potato shortage similar to the earlier famine. Demanding landlords evicted tenants from the rocky land around Knock.

In 1867, Archdeacon[1] Cavanagh became pastor of the local parish church, St. John the Baptist. In 1878, a storm had partially destroyed the roof and statues in the church, and Archdeacon Cavanagh promptly had the roof repaired and ordered replacement statues. One new statue was of Our Lady of Lourdes, thus indicating that Knock parishioners knew about the 1858 apparition of the Virgin Mary in Lourdes.

Painting of Our Lady's visit to Knock in the Church of the Apparition

The Apparition

Extraordinary events in Knock began in August 1879, a week after the feast of Our Lady's Assumption. Rain had poured down steadily on the evening of Thursday, August 21, when Mary McLoughlin, Archdeacon Cavanagh's housekeeper, left the rectory to visit her friend Margaret Byrne. Mary noticed strange figures and a white light outside the church, but assumed they were more statues that the Archdeacon had purchased.

A Mrs. Carty had also seen the "statues" while passing the church. Margaret Byrne, the younger daughter of Mary McLoughlin's friend, also saw something luminous at the south wall while locking the church around 7:30 P.M., but she did not investigate.

---

1. An archdeacon was a priest who had authority from the bishop to administer part of the diocese, similar to a vicar-general today.

Mary McLoughlin left Margaret Byrne's home to return to the rectory around 8:00 P.M., accompanied by Mary Byrne, Margaret's elder daughter. As they approached the church grounds in the rain, Mary Byrne noticed the figures. "When did the Archdeacon put new statues there?" she asked the housekeeper. But as they approached the church wall, a brilliant light appeared. The figures the two women saw couldn't be statues. They were moving!

A life-size Blessed Virgin stood in mid-air, two feet above the tall grass by the church. St. Joseph and St. John the Evangelist appeared slightly smaller. The women had recognized St. John from a statue in a church in Lechanvy. "Quick, call your family!" the housekeeper told Mary Byrne. Soon the Byrne family and a dozen others gathered to see the apparition for another hour.

Patrick Walsh, an elderly farmer, later testified that he saw a brilliant stationary light over the church while returning home from his fields around 9:00 P.M. He thought it might be a fire. Because he also saw the light at some distance from the group, mass hallucination cannot explain the phenomena.

The visionaries that night included the children John Curry, Catherine Murray and Patrick Hill; members of the Byrne family, Margaret, Patrick, Dominick Sr., Dominick Jr. and Mary; Mary

Apparition scene in the Apparition Gable Chapel

McLoughlin; Patrick Walsh; Bridget Trench; Mrs. Hugh Flatley, Judith Campbell and John Durkan. These witnesses ranged in age from six to seventy-five.

Behind the three figures dressed in dazzling white, the visionaries also saw an altar where the Lamb of God, symbolizing Jesus, stood before a large cross. A ring of white angels surrounded the Lamb. Our Lady gazed at the heavens as if in prayer. She wore a crown adorned with glittering crosses, and a beautiful rose where the crown touched her brow. The Virgin held her extended hands upward, portraying her role as Advocate interceding with God for those who pray for her help.

Despite the downpour, Mary McLoughlin and the others noticed that not one drop of rain touched the three figures. She also saw that the ground beneath the figures was dry, as was the church wall.

A bearded St. Joseph, his gray head bowed in respect, stood to the right of Our Lady. St. John appeared as a young man wearing a bishop's miter or cap and dressed in priestly vestments. He held an open book in his left hand while his right was raised as in preaching, thus representing the teaching Church. None of the three figures spoke.

The fountains at Knock

Around 11:00 P.M., the elderly Bridget Trench went to embrace the Virgin's feet, but found her arms empty. The figures vanished soon after, and the crowd then began to disperse.

Stained glass window in the Church of the Apparition

The meaning of the apparition seems to lie in the symbolism of the altar, the lamb and the cross. The other two figures are also symbolic—St. Joseph as protector of the Church and families, and St. John as indicating the role of the priest, the importance of the Mass, and the central place of the Scriptures.

At first the Archdeacon doubted Mary McLoughlin's story of the vision, thinking she may have taken too much of a stimulant for an illness she suffered. He refused to return to the church with his housekeeper that evening.

But the Archdeacon heard similar stories at Mass the next day from other parishioners who felt they had been blessed because of their pastor's holiness and his devotion to the Virgin Mary. The Archdeacon soon became a firm believer in the apparition.

The Visionaries after the Apparition

Dominick and Margaret Byrne and their niece Catherine Murray died a few years after the apparition. So did Patrick Walsh, the elderly farmer, and Bridget Trench, the woman who had tried to hug the Virgin Mary. Archdeacon Cavanagh died in 1897 on the Feast of the Immaculate Conception. Mary Byrne died in 1936 at the age of eighty-two. Patrick Hill went to the United States and died in Boston around 1927. John Curry also went to America. Patrick Byrne lived the longest of all the witnesses.

The Pietà in the Church of the Apparition

Miraculous Cures

Miraculous cures were reported within weeks of the Knock apparition. Some persons—who were deaf, blind, lame, paralyzed or sick with tuberculosis or cancer—were said to have been cured instantly after drinking water in which scraps of cement from the church wall had been dissolved. The Archdeacon had to encase the lower wall in wooden sheathing for fear that the constant scraping away of cement would collapse it. Archdeacon Cavanagh documented these original cures in his diary, published in 1880.

The Recognition Process

Two commissions of inquiry—in 1879 and 1936—have investigated the Knock apparitions. Six weeks after the apparition, Archbishop John McHale of Tuam established a diocesan commission of nine priests to officially investigate what happened at Knock. Fifteen witnesses of the apparition gave signed testimonies; the commission declared each testimony trustworthy. Archbishop McHale, then ninety and in poor health, made no official statement on Knock, but is reported to have said, "…it is a great blessing to the poor people of the West, in their wretchedness and misery and suffering, that the Blessed Virgin, Mother of God has appeared among them."

In 1929, the new Archbishop of Tuam, Archbishop Gilmartin, joined a pilgrimage to Knock. He stated that people could make up their own minds about Knock since the Church had made no official decision after the 1879 commission. In 1936 he set up a second commission to examine the three surviving witnesses of the apparition: Mary Byrne, Patrick Byrne and John Curry. All confirmed their original statements made in 1879. The commission concluded that they had given reliable testimony.

The first organized pilgrimage to the Knock shrine took place in 1880 when fifty pilgrims from Limerick traveled to Knock by horse-drawn cart. A pilgrimage from Cork donated a beautiful high altar to the old church in 1879. It depicts the Pietà, as Jesus lay in the arms of Our Blessed Lady after having been taken from the cross. Many other pilgrimages followed in the 1880s, some with archbishops from other countries, including Canada and Australia.

The golden rose displayed in the old church

Many other bishops have made personal pilgrimages to the shrine, thus giving it credibility. Pope John Paul II made a pilgrimage to Knock in 1979, the centenary year. A crowd of five hundred thousand welcomed the Pope, who presented a golden rose and two beautiful mosaics to the basilica. The golden rose has historically been given by the Pope to commemorate a special event. In this case it symbolizes the rose that Mary wore during her Knock appearance. Today, over one million pilgrims visit Knock annually. Although the Knock apparition site has never been officially approved, the Church has encouraged devotion there, thus granting unofficial approval.

The Shrine

The original church of the apparition stands today. A white marble exhibit of the apparition scene, enclosed by plate glass, stands by its gable wall. The center of attention is neither Mary, nor Joseph, nor John the Evangelist, but the cross and the lamb, symbolic of Christ.

On June 6, 1974, Pope Paul VI blessed the foundation stone to begin construction of the new church of Our Lady, Queen of Ireland. Dedicated on July 1, 1976, it was raised to the status of a basilica during the pilgrimage of Pope John Paul II in 1979.

The basilica accommodates twenty thousand people and is open all year, but holds regular services only from May to October. The original church holds services year-round. The shrine has daily Masses, anointing of the sick, and the stations of the cross. A public novena, beginning with Mass in the basilica followed by a candlelight procession, takes place nightly from August 14 to August 22. Church and State dignitaries from around the world attend the annual feast of Our Lady of Knock on August 21.

Perpetual adoration of the Eucharist takes place in a special chapel at the shrine with all-night vigils held monthly. The circular basilica holds the *Icon of Knock* made by Desmond Kyne, depicting the Blessed Virgin and the Lamb of God against a background of Celtic symbols.

Tapestry of the apparition in the new basilica

The new basilica of Knock

Crucifixion scene at Knock

Icon of Knock in the new basilica

In 1957, the Apparition Church at Knock became affiliated with the Basilica of St. Mary Major in Rome. In 1971, permission was granted to the Knock shrine to carry out the anointing of the sick.

Planning a Pilgrimage

Ireland, the Emerald Isle, is known for the richness of its culture. Ireland offers lush greenness, shamrocks, the Blarney stone, harps, limericks, the lakes of Killarney, the Rock of Cashel, the waterways of Cork, Waterford crystal, salmon fishing in Galway, the craggy coastlines of Connemara and County Sligo's seaside resorts.

Most pilgrims will start in Dublin, the capital and largest city with a population of five hundred thousand. Famous sites in Dublin include Trinity College, St. Patrick's and Christ Church Cathedrals, the National Museum, the National Gallery and Dublin Castle.

An airport now serves Knock with flights from Dublin and Sligo, besides some international flights. Daily bus transport is available from Dublin, Sligo, Westport, Castlebar and Claremorris. Pilgrims can travel by train from Dublin to nearby Sligo and Westport.

Among the facilities near the Knock shrine are the Blessed Sacrament Chapel, the new Chapel of Reconciliation, St. Brigid's and St. Mary's Hostels, St. Joseph's Rest Home for Invalids, a folk museum, a family life center and a marriage bureau. Pilgrims can find solitude and tranquillity in a lush green park with winding paths adjacent to the basilica.

Westport, Ireland

From Knock, one can drive along winding country roads through moorland and farmers' fields to the coastal towns of Newport and Westport, overlooking Clew Bay, studded with hundreds of islands. To the south is Croagh Patrick. On the last Sunday of July, twenty-five thousand pilgrims climb to its summit to honor St. Patrick.

CHAPTER EIGHT

Our Lady of the Rosary

Fatima, Portugal (1917)

Stained glass window of the miracle of the sun

Summary

The Angel of Peace appeared three times to Lucia dos Santos and her cousins Francisco and Jacinta Marto in Fatima, Portugal, in 1916. The next year, the Blessed Virgin appeared monthly to the three children from May to October. From 1926 to 1929, Lucia, then a religious, received further messages from Mary who asked for devotion to her Immaculate Heart and for the consecration of Russia.

The Blessed Virgin who appeared in Fatima is known as Our Lady of the Rosary—the title she gave the children during her last appearance. Millions of pilgrims visit Fatima today. Inspired by its message, millions more devote themselves to the Immaculate Heart and to prayer and penance as the Blessed Virgin requested.

The Historical Context

World War I was already underway when Portugal declared war on Germany in March 1916. The assassination of King Carlos six years earlier had ended Portugal's monarchy. The new republican government openly opposed religion.

The agricultural village of Fatima is seventy miles north of Lisbon in the diocese of Leiria. It is named after Mohammed's sister, reflecting the Moorish influence in Iberia. The families of Lucia dos Santos and her cousins lived in the tiny hamlet of Aljustrel, half a mile south of Fatima. The youngest of seven children, Lucia was nine years old in 1916. She tended the family's sheep along with her cousin Francisco Marto, eight, and his sister,

The Dos Santos home

A well at Aljustrel

Jacinta Marto, six. All attended the village church, St. Anthony's, in Fatima, one and a half miles from the current Chapel of the Apparitions. At the time, Fatima's population was only 2,600.

Francisco liked to describe the sun as Our Lord's lamp, the moon as Our Lady's lamp, and the stars as the lamps of the angels. He preferred Our Lord's lamp because of the sun's rays, but Jacinta preferred Our Lady's lamp because she could look at it without hurting her eyes.

The Apparition

That spring the three children took their sheep to the Chousa Velha, property of Lucia's father, at the foot of Loca de Cabeço, a rocky promontory west of Aljustrel. A steady drizzle forced the children to take shelter in a cave. The shower soon passed and the sun shone again. Then a strong wind began to shake the olive trees.

Looking up, the children saw a figure of a young man coming toward them above the trees, his skin transparent as crystal.

"Do not be afraid. I am the Angel of Peace," the angel told the children. "Pray with me." The angel knelt and bowed until his forehead touched the ground. He had the children repeat, "My God, I believe, I adore, I hope, and I love you. I ask pardon of you for those who do not believe, do not adore, do not hope, and do not love you." The angel then rose and bid the children farewell, saying, "Pray thus. The hearts of Jesus and Mary are attentive to the voice of your petitions."

The angel appeared a second time in the summer when the children were playing at the well in the garden of Lucia's parents in Aljustrel. "Pray, pray very much," the angel told them. "The most holy hearts of Jesus and Mary have designs of mercy on you. Offer prayers and sacrifices constantly to the Most High."

The children asked how to make sacrifices. "Make a sacrifice of everything you can, and offer it to God as an act of reparation for sins and in supplication for the conversion of sinners," the angel told them. "You will thus bring peace to your country. I am its guardian angel, the angel of Portugal." The angel also encouraged them to offer to God whatever sufferings they had to deal with.

Dazzling and resplendent, the angel appeared a third and final time to the children that fall. While grazing their sheep near an olive grove called Pregueira, they were reciting the prayer the angel had taught them during his first appearance.

Statue of the Angel of Peace near Aljustrel

Stained glass window depicting the Holy Eucharist

An extraordinary light suddenly shone upon the children. The angel held a chalice in his left hand; his other hand suspended the Host above it. A few drops of blood fell from the Host into the chalice. The angel left the chalice suspended in the air, knelt by the children, and had them repeat three times:

"Most Holy Trinity, Father, Son, and Holy Spirit, I adore you profoundly, and I offer you the most precious body, blood, soul and divinity of Jesus Christ, present in all the tabernacles of the world, in reparation for the outrages, sacrileges and indifference by which

Painting of Mary, Queen of the Universe

he is offended. And through the infinite merits of his most Sacred Heart, and the Immaculate Heart of Mary, I beg of you the conversion of poor sinners."

The angel took the chalice and the Host in his hands. He gave the Sacred Host to Lucia and shared the blood from the chalice between Jacinta and Francisco, saying, "Take and drink the Body and Blood of Jesus Christ, horribly outraged by ungrateful men. Make reparation for their crimes and console your God."

On May 13, 1917, a brilliant light flashed as the children again tended their sheep in the Cova da Iria (Cove of Irene), a pasture belonging to Lucia's father. Above the branches of a small holm oak tree, three feet high, they saw a beautiful Lady dressed in white. She radiated an intense light.

"Do not be afraid," the Lady told the children. "I am from heaven." She told the children to come to the same spot on the thirteenth day of each month for six successive months. Lucia asked if she and her cousins would go to heaven, and the Lady assured her that they would. Then the lady asked if they would be willing to offer themselves to God, along with any sufferings they would experience, in reparation for sins and for the conversion of sinners.

The children said yes. The Lady then told them that the grace of God would sustain and comfort them.

Opening her hands for the first time, Mary revealed an intense light whose rays streamed from her hands, penetrating the children's hearts and souls, making them see themselves in God.

"Pray the rosary every day to obtain peace for the world and the end of the war," the Lady said. She then began to rise toward the east. The surrounding light opened a path before her, and the children felt that heaven opened as the Lady disappeared into the immensity of space.

The children agreed among themselves to tell no one of their experience, but Jacinta felt so excited she told her family that evening. The news spread quickly around the village. When Lucia's

Mary's Immaculate Heart stained glass window

family heard it, they dismissed the story. A period of constant ridicule, taunting and punishment—even beatings—began for Lucia. The local priest suggested to her that she might have witnessed Satan's work. While Lucia's parents doubted, her cousins' parents, especially their father, Manuel Marto, supported them.

The children were praying the rosary when they saw the flash again on June 13, 1917, the feast of St. Anthony. Our Lady said she would soon take Jacinta and Francisco to heaven, but Jesus wanted Lucia to stay in the world and establish devotion to Mary's Immaculate Heart. Lucia asked sadly if she would be alone. "No, my daughter," Our Lady replied. "Do not lose heart. I will never forsake you. My Immaculate Heart will be your refuge, and the way that will lead you to God."

Our Lady opened her hands so that the rays of the immense light shone on the children for the second time. They saw themselves in the light, immersed in God. Jacinta and Francisco seemed to be in the part of the light rising toward heaven, while Lucia was in the part pouring down on earth. Our Lady held a heart encircled and

Spinning sun and cross stained glass window

pierced by thorns in the palm of her right hand. The children understood it was Mary's Immaculate Heart.

On July 13 the children returned to the Cova with a large crowd. Our Lady told them: "Sacrifice yourselves for sinners and say many times, especially whenever you make some sacrifice: 'O Jesus, this is for the love of you, for the conversion of sinners, and in reparation for the sins committed against the Immaculate Heart of Mary.'"

Our Lady then opened her hands, and rays of light seemed to penetrate the earth. The children saw a vision of hell that horrified them.

"You have seen hell, where the souls of poor sinners go," Mary told the children. "To save them, God wishes to establish devotion to my Immaculate Heart in the world. If what I say to you is done, many souls will be saved and there will be peace. The war will end. But if people do not cease offending God, a worse war will break out during the pontificate of Pius XI. When you see a night illuminated by an unknown light, know this is the great sign given you by God that he is about to punish the world for its crimes by means of war, famine and persecutions of the Church and of the Holy Father.[2]

2. An extraordinary aurora borealis occurred on January 25, 1938, shortly before the outbreak of World War II. Germany occupied Austria soon after.

*Statue of Our Lady in the
Chapel of the Apparition*

"To prevent this, I have come to ask for the consecration of Russia to my Immaculate Heart, and the Communion of reparation on the First Saturdays. If my requests are heeded, Russia will be converted and there will be peace. If not, Russia will spread her errors throughout the world, causing wars and persecutions of the Church. The good will be martyred. The Holy Father will have much to suffer. Various nations will be annihilated. In the end, my Immaculate Heart will triumph. The Holy Father will consecrate Russia to me and she will be converted, and a period of peace will be granted to the world."

After the apparition on July 13, Jacinta, while playing at the well, saw a vision of the Pope kneeling before a table and crying. He went to the door of the house, but found people cursing him and throwing stones. Jacinta concluded it meant we should pray for the Holy Father.

A crowd of eighteen thousand had gathered at the Cova da Iria on August 13, but the children could not appear because Arturo de Oliveira Santos, the Administrator of Ourém and a blacksmith by trade, had imprisoned them for two days. An anti-cleric, he even threatened to drop the children in boiling oil, but they reaffirmed their story.

On August 19, Our Lady appeared at Valinhos and told the three children she wanted a chapel constructed there. She also told them to continue praying the rosary and to make sacrifices for sinners.

On September 13, a luminous globe suddenly appeared before a crowd of thirty thousand. Our Lady told the children a great miracle would occur in October, and they should pray the rosary so the war would end. She said they would see the Lord in October, as well as Our Lady of Sorrows and Our Lady of Mount Carmel. She also told them St. Joseph would appear with the Child Jesus to bless the world, and God was pleased with their sacrifices.

The story of Our Lady's appearances had spread through Portugal. A major storm raged across Europe the night of October 12. The next day, a crowd of seventy thousand waded through the muddy fields to witness the miracle. The familiar flash of light signaled Our Lady's arrival to the children. "I am the Lady of the Rosary," she told them, then opened her hands and rays of light extended toward the sun.

The miracle was about to begin. The sun grew pale, then lost its color and changed to a silver disk the people could gaze at without hurting their eyes. Rays of red, orange, yellow, green, blue—all the colors of the spectrum—suddenly shot out in all directions and the sun seemed to spin on its axis, like a kaleidoscope. It stopped, then began its mad dance twice more. The sun then tore loose from

Chapel of the Apparition

its place in the heavens and hurled close to earth, zigzagging across the skies. The crowd thought the world would end. People screamed and cried for mercy.

Suddenly, the silver disk stopped plunging downward, as if halted by an invisible heavenly hand. The sun returned to its usual position, shining with its normal brilliancy. People could no longer look at it directly. The rain-soaked clothes of the crowd dried instantly.

The children saw, in heavenly tableaus, visions of the mysteries of the rosary, then of the Holy Family. St. Joseph, dressed in white and holding on his arm the Child who was dressed in red, appeared first. Our Lady, to his right, wore a blue mantle. St. Joseph traced the sign of the cross and blessed the crowds. Then Lucia saw the Blessed Virgin, dressed in purple, as Our Lady of Sorrows on Good Friday. Beside her stood her divine Son, vested in red, and grieving as when he had met her on the way to Calvary. Mary then appeared alone in the brown robes of Our Lady of Mount Carmel, crowned as Queen of Heaven, with what appeared to be a scapular falling from her hand.

The Visionaries after the Apparition

Francisco Marto fell victim to an influenza epidemic that swept Europe. He died at age ten of bronchial pneumonia on April 4, 1919. His sister, Jacinta Marto, also suffered bouts of influenza and developed purulent pleurisy. She was taken to St. Augustina Hospital in Ourém, then to the Hospital of Dona Stefania in Lisbon. Only nine years old, she died there alone on February 20, 1920, after a major operation to remove two infected ribs. Mary had earlier told Jacinta she would

Resting place of Jacinta Marto in the basilica

die alone in a dark place, but to have courage because she would come to personally take her to heaven. The prediction had now been fulfilled. The memoirs of Lucia dos Santos pay tribute to the suffering Jacinta willingly accepted in response to Mary's message.

Jacinta's room

On instructions from her bishop, Lucia dos Santos wrote a series of memoirs in 1935, 1937 and 1941. She described the visits of the Angel of Peace in 1916 and later events at Fatima, as well as visions of Mary and Christ that she had from 1925 to 1929.

In 1921, Lucia made a farewell visit to the initial Chapel of the Apparitions, built in 1917 at the Cova. She was fourteen years old when she left Aljustrel and arrived at the school of the Sisters of St. Dorothy at Vilar, now a suburb of Porto, on June 17, 1921. The bishop had arranged for her to assume a different identity at the school until the Church affirmed the apparitions. She remained in Porto for four years as a boarding student.

At age eighteen, Lucia entered the Dorothean Sisters in Túy, Spain, near the Portuguese border. She was sent to the convent at Pontevedra, Spain (thirty miles from the famous pilgrimage site of Santiago de Compostela) where she stayed as a postulant from October 1925 to July 1926.

While there, Lucia had an apparition of the Virgin Mary and the Child Jesus on December 10, 1925. Mary told her:

> Look, my daughter, at my heart surrounded with thorns with which ungrateful persons pierce me by their blasphemies and ingratitude. You at least try to console me. I promise to assist at the hour of death, with the graces necessary for salvation, all those who shall, on the first Saturday of five consecutive months, confess, receive Holy Communion, recite five decades of the rosary, and keep me company for fifteen minutes while meditating on the mysteries of the rosary, with the intent to make reparation to me.

In February 1926 the Child Jesus appeared again in Pontevedra and invited Lucia to spread devotion to the Immaculate Heart of Mary. Sister Lucia made her vows in Túy on October 3, 1928, and on June 13, 1929, she had a vision of the Holy Trinity. In 1948 Lucia transferred to the more austere cloister of the Carmelite nuns in Coimbra, Portugal. There, she is known as Sister Maria Lucia of the Immaculate Heart. As of 1999 she is ninety-two years old and still living as a Carmelite in Coimbra.

The Recognition Process

On October 13, 1930, José Alves Correia da Silva, the bishop of Leiria where Fatima and Aljustrel are located, declared the apparitions worthy of belief.

Pope Pius XII consecrated nations to the Immaculate Heart of Mary in a radio message to the entire world, but especially to Portugal and the pilgrims gathered at Fatima, on October 13, 1942, twenty-five years after the apparitions.

Pope Paul VI visited Fatima on May 13, 1967, the fiftieth anniversary of the apparitions. There, he presented a golden rose to the sanctuary and met Lucia, who had permission to visit Fatima for this special occasion. Pope John Paul II visited Fatima on May 13, 1982, sixty-five years after the apparitions. He, too, met Lucia. The Pope, who had survived an assassin's bullet a year before, believed he owed his life to the Immaculate Heart of Mary. Pope John Paul II later consecrated the world to Mary's Immaculate Heart.

On May 13, 1989, Pope John Paul II declared Jacinta and Francisco had lived lives of heroic virtue and are now Venerable Servants of God. This is the first step toward beatification and canonization in the Catholic Church. In January 1999, the Congregation for the Causes of Saints accepted the miracle required for their beatification. It involves the healing of Maria Emilia Santos, who had been bedridden for twenty years. Her cure in 1987 of tuberculosis was obtained through the intercession of Jacinta and Francisco.

In the spring of 2000, Jacinta and Francisco were beatified in Rome, making them the two youngest "Blesseds" in the history of the Church.

The Shrine

A twelve-foot high wooden arch with two lanterns was built on the apparition site in 1917. Construction of the Chapel of the Apparitions, called the *capelhina,* began on August 6, 1918, the feast of the Transfiguration. In 1920, one of Portugal's finest sculptors, José Ferreira Thedim, completed a statue of Our Lady as she appeared at the Cova, holding a rosary in her joined hands. The statue was carved from Brazilian cedar and painted white and gold. In 1921, Bishop da Silva used donations from pilgrims to purchase thirty acres of land at the Cova da Iria.

Vandals dynamited the chapel during the night of March 6, 1922. Four bombs destroyed its roof, but the chapel was immedi-

Panorama of the Fatima Basilica

Fountains near the basilica

Entrance to the esplanade

ately restored and enlarged. The original statue of Our Lady of Fatima was not damaged and still stands in front of the *capelhina,* on the exact spot where Mary appeared. Pilgrims can drink spring water from a row of faucets near the chapel.

Across from the *capelhina* is the Adoration Chapel, where perpetual adoration of the Blessed Sacrament takes place. Pilgrims can find there a place for quiet prayer and reflection.

The Basilica of Our Lady, Queen of the Holy Rosary was dedicated on October 7, 1953. Bishop da Silva organized the project, which took twenty-five years to complete. Its tower, 215

Candles symbolizing divine light

feet high, is topped by a seven-ton bronze crown and a large crystal cross. The basilica's fifteen altars correspond to the fifteen decades of the rosary. Francisco and Jacinta are entombed in a side chapel. A beautiful stained glass window depicts the miracle of the sun. Originally in the Adoration Chapel, the window has now been moved to another sanctuary building.

To the right of the basilica stands the Chapel of Reconciliation, where pilgrims can receive the sacrament of Reconciliation. Confessions are heard in many languages.

The grounds of the shrine also have outdoor stations of the cross donated by the people of Hungary. Built along a stone path, the stations lead to a hill where the crucifixion scene is represented by several large statues. From the top of the hill one has a magnificent view of the surrounding area. A chapel dedicated to St. Stephen of Hungary is found at the bottom of the hill.

Candlelight processions are held at night. Hundreds of thousands of pilgrims come to Fatima on the thirteenth of each month from May to October. As many as one million attend the May celebrations. A tall cross at the sanctuary's entrance beckons the pilgrim to prayer and penance. Many pilgrims, as an act of penance, cross the entire esplanade on their knees. Near the Cova entrance is a statue of Pope Paul, kneeling and looking toward the basilica.

On August 13, 1994, the Bishop of Leiria-Fatima dedicated a glass-encased monument holding a large column of the Berlin Wall.

The Paul VI Pastoral Center

A plaque explains the connection between the Fatima message and the fall of communism.

Work on a hospital began at the sanctuary in 1924. A Medical Bureau was established in 1926 to assist the sick and examine cures considered miraculous.

A new health care facility known as the Sanctuary Hospice of Our Lady of Sorrows was dedicated on October 13, 1994.

Also at the sanctuary is the Pius XII Monastery, an English speaking community dedicated to the perpetual rosary; the seminary of the Missionaries of the Divine Word; and the seminary of the Consolata Missionaries. The international headquarters (*Domus Pacis*) of the Blue Army, which promotes the message of Fatima, is located by the sanctuary and houses a residence for pilgrims. The Paul VI Pastoral Center, with its huge amphitheater, is nearby.

At the Cabeço, the pilgrim will find statues of the children before the Angel of Peace who holds a host and chalice.

The official sanctuary bulletin is entitled *Voz da Fatima,* or the Voice of Fatima.

Planning a Pilgrimage

The trip from Lisbon to Fatima takes about two hours by bus, available daily year-round. Estramada Province, where Fatima is located, has many tourist attractions including historical monuments, lovely beaches, thermal springs and underground caves.

The pilgrim could visit the Marian shrines at Batalha, Alcobaça and Nazaré, all relatively near Fatima. Construction of the Gothic monastery of St. Mary of Victory began in 1387 in Batalha after the Portuguese defeated Spain in battle. Inside its church is the statue of Our Lady of Victory, patroness of the monastery.

The monastery of Santa Maria de Alcobaça dates to 1151, when the king of Portugal invited St. Bernard and his monks from Cîteaux, France, to found a monastery in Portugal. The church at the monastery, the largest in Portugal, is of Romantic style with Gothic influence, and was dedicated in 1157. The abbey at Alcobaça, with its extensive library of manuscripts, was Portugal's main center of learning for centuries. The statue of Our Lady of Penha dates from the 14th century.

Nazaré, a delightful seaside resort and fishing village, lies thirty-five miles west of Fatima. The oldest religious image in Portugal, the statue of Our Lady of Nazaré, also called Our Lady of the Milk, is kept in the Church of Our Lady of Nazaré, built in 1377. Vasco de Gama visited the church before he left for India; so did St. Francis Xavier before setting off for the Orient.

CHAPTER NINE

The Merciful Jesus

KRAKOW, POLAND (1931)

Image of Divine Mercy in
St. Casimir's Church

Summary

God called Sister Faustina Kowalska to a unique mission—a mission of mercy. Through her efforts, a greater trust in Divine Mercy has spread throughout the world. Sister Faustina spent thirteen years in the Congregation of the Sisters of Our Lady of Mercy, living in various cities including Warsaw, Plock, Vilnius and Krakow. A cook, gardener and gatekeeper, Sister Faustina had a vision of the Merciful Jesus in 1931 at a convent in Poland. Jesus revealed to her the Divine Mercy message and devotion.

This devotion includes venerating the image of Divine Mercy, praying the chaplet of Divine Mercy, celebrating the Feast of Mercy on the Sunday after Easter, and recalling Christ's passion, especially at three o'clock. The essence of being an apostle of mercy is living with an attitude of trust in God's mercy and practicing active mercy toward others.

Sister Faustina suffered from tuberculosis and died in Krakow when she was thirty-three. Pope John Paul II beatified her in 1993 and canonized her in 2000.

The Historical Context

The Polish nation, formed in 962 and composed of Slav tribes, converted to Christianity under Mieszko in 966. The second oldest university after Prague in Eastern Europe was founded in Krakow in 1364. Under the two hundred-year reign of the Jagiellon dynasty, Poland by the mid-16th century had expanded from the Baltic to the Black Sea. Lithuania was merged with Poland in 1569. By the 17th century, Poland faced attacks from Sweden and Russia. In three partitions in the 18th century, Poland lost much territory to Prussia, Russia and Austria.

The Poland where Sister Faustina lived had only recently regained its independence after the armistice concluding World War I. The new republic established in 1918 lasted only until the Nazis invaded Poland on September 1, 1939, igniting World War II.

Sister Faustina was born on August 25, 1905, in the Polish village of Glogowiec near the textile city of Lodz. Two days later, she was baptized Helena in the parish church of Swinice Warckie. Helena was the third of ten children. Her father, Stanislaus Kowalski, ran a farm and supplemented his income with carpentry. Her hard-working mother Marianna tended to the needs of the large family and helped with the farm work when possible.

From an early age, Helena was drawn to God and prayer. By seven, she felt God's call inviting her to a life of holiness. She received the sacraments of Reconciliation and Holy Communion

Sister Faustina's home (Glogowiec, Poland)

Church in Aleksandrow, Poland

when she was nine, at the parish church of St. Casimir at Swinice, two kilometers from her home. Sometime in 1922, Helena received the sacrament of Confirmation in Aleksandrow, near Lodz.

St. Stanislaus Kostka (Lodz)

World War I and the Russian occupation of Poland had forced schools to close. Helena was twelve before she could enter elementary school in Swinice in 1917. After only three years, she and the other older students had to leave school to make room for younger children.

After leaving school, Helena worked at home until 1921 helping her mother with the daily chores. Then she worked as a housemaid for a neighbor's sister who lived in Aleksandrow. She worked during the day and prayed at night, as her longing for God increased. After a year, she left her job and told her parents she wanted to enter a convent. But they denied permission because they could not afford the dowry and trousseau required to enter.

In 1922, when she was seventeen, Helena went to live with cousins in Lodz. She worked for friends of the family and attended Mass daily. She increasingly felt the desire to enter religious life, but her parents still refused permission. While working as a maid and caring for children from another family, she fasted on Wednesdays, Fridays and Saturdays.

At a dance in Lodz in 1924, Helena had a vision, seeing Jesus next to her. He asked her, "How long shall I put up with you and how long will you keep putting Me off?" (*The Diary of Sister Faustina Kowalska,* Message #9). Helena left the dance and went to the Cathedral of St. Stanislaus Kostka to pray for the Lord's guidance. A voice told her, "Go at once to Warsaw; you will enter a convent there" (*Diary,* 10).

With only the clothes she was wearing, Helena took the train to Warsaw. Despite her faith, she felt frightened because she knew no one there. She prayed to Mary for guidance and later went to the Church of St. James (St. Jakok) in Ochota, a southern suburb of Warsaw. A voice told her to tell the priest what had happened and he would advise her about what to do next. The priest referred Helena to a family where she could stay until she found a convent that would accept her.

Helena knocked on one convent door after another until she was accepted by the Sisters of Our Lady of Mercy. But Helena could not enter for another year, because she had to work to pay for the wardrobe. Finally, on August 1, 1925, the eve of the Feast of Our Lady of the Angels, Helena Kowalska entered the convent.

After six months in Warsaw, Helena was transferred to Krakow at the beginning of 1926, where she remained for the duration of her post-ulancy and novitiate (a

St. Jakok's Church (Warsaw)

time of testing one's vocation and learning about the religious life and vows). There, she learned more about this order originally founded in Laval, France in 1818. When Helena received the habit and white veil, she also took a new name to symbolize the beginning of her new life. She was given the name Sister Mary Faustina, and became known simply as Sister Faustina, meaning the fortunate, happy or blessed one.

Convent at 29 Grybo Street (Vilnius)

During the first year of her novitiate, she underwent a trying six month period of interior desolation. She found no consolation in prayer and her doubts increased. She made a novena to St. Thérèse of the Child Jesus. In a dream, St. Thérèse said that she also had suffered greatly, and encouraged Sister Faustina to trust God more. St. Thérèse told her she would go to heaven and become a saint.

After Sister Faustina made her profession of vows in 1928, she became a cook in the same convent where she had been a postulant. The next year Sister Faustina was sent to a convent in Vilnius, the capital of Lithuania, then under Polish rule. Soon after, she was sent to Plock in Poland.

The Apparition

While in Plock, Sister Faustina received the first of many revelations concerning her mission to be a messenger of Divine Mercy. In her room on the evening of February 22, 1931, she saw Jesus clothed in a white garment. He held one hand to his chest while raising his other hand in blessing. Sister Faustina saw two large rays, one pale, the other red, radiating from his robe.

Jesus told her, "Paint an image according to the pattern you see, with the signature: Jesus, I trust in You. I desire that this image be venerated, first in your chapel, and [then] throughout the world. I promise that the soul that will venerate this image will not perish" (*Diary,* 47, 48).

*Painting of Sister Faustina
(Wronia Street, Krakow)*

Both Sister Faustina's confessor and her superior downplayed this message and did nothing to help her get the image painted. While at a retreat in Warsaw, another confessor, Rev. Edmund Elter, reassured Sister Faustina she was on the right path. Sister Faustina then received a new assignment in Vilnius.

From 1933 to 1936 Sister Faustina lived in Vilnius, where she worked as a gardener. At her first confession in the Vilnius convent, she met Fr. Michael Sopocko, the pastor of St. Michael's Church. He became Sister Faustina's spiritual director and was gradually convinced that the gifts of the Holy Spirit were at work in her. He asked her to record her experiences in a diary that Sister Faustina continued to write until poor health prevented it.

In June 1934 Fr. Sopocko had Eugene Kazimierowski paint an image of Divine Mercy based on Sister Faustina's instructions, but it disappointed her. The first public exposition of the painting was held for three days in 1935, beginning on the Sunday after Easter. In 1937 Kazimierowski's painting was placed in the Bernardine Sisters' convent in Vilnius, near St. Michael's Church where Fr. Sopocko was pastor. Now it hangs in the Church of the Holy Spirit on Dominican Street in Vilnius.

In 1931 Jesus first told Sister Faustina of his wish to have the Feast of Divine Mercy instituted. "I desire that there be a Feast of Mercy. I want this image...to be solemnly blessed on the first Sunday after Easter; that Sunday is to be the Feast of Mercy" (*Diary*, 49). Jesus referred to this request during fourteen of the apparitions.

First painting of Divine Mercy by Eugene Kazimierowski

Jesus later told Sister Faustina: "The two rays denote Blood and Water. The pale ray stands for the Water which makes souls righteous. The red ray stands for the Blood that is the life of souls.... These two rays issued forth from the very depths of My tender mercy when My agonized Heart was opened by a lance on the Cross.... Happy is the one who will dwell in their shelter, for the just hand of God shall not lay hold of him" (*Diary*, 299).

Jesus asked that people celebrate the feast by receiving the sacraments of Reconciliation and the Eucharist, and by doing deeds of mercy.

On September 13, 1935, Sister Faustina received the words of the chaplet during a vision when she was alone in her room. Using words she heard from an interior voice, she pleaded with God for the world and understood that this prayer had great power to obtain God's mercy for sinful people (cf. *Diary*, 474).

When Sister Faustina entered the convent chapel the next day, she heard an interior voice say:

> Every time you enter the chapel, immediately recite the prayer which I taught you yesterday.... You will recite it for nine days, on the beads of the rosary, in the following manner:

First of all, you will say one "Our Father" and "Hail Mary" and the "I believe in God." Then on the "Our Father" beads you will say the following words: "Eternal Father, I offer You the Body and Blood, Soul and Divinity of Your dearly beloved Son, Our Lord Jesus Christ, in atonement for our sins and those of the whole world." On the "Hail Mary" beads you will say the following words: "For the sake of His sorrowful Passion have mercy on us and on the whole world." In conclusion, three times you will recite these words: "Holy God, Holy Mighty One, Holy Immortal One, have mercy on us and on the whole world" (*Diary,* 476).

In 1936 Fr. Sopocko had a Krakow publishing company print a prayer card with the Divine Mercy image on one side and the chaplet prayers on its reverse.

Sister Faustina moved permanently to Krakow in March 1936. The following September, Jesus told her: "Say unceasingly the chaplet that I have taught you. Whoever will recite it will receive great mercy at the hour of death. Priests will recommend it to sinners as their last hope of salvation. Even if there were a sinner most hardened, if he were to recite this chaplet only once, he would receive grace from My infinite mercy. I desire that the whole world know My infinite mercy. I desire to grant unimaginable graces to those souls who trust in My mercy" (*Diary,* 687).

Kazimierowski painting in Holy Spirit Church (Vilnius)

On Good Friday, 1937, Our Lady told Sister Faustina that the chaplet of Divine Mercy should be prayed as a novena before the Feast of Mercy, starting on Good Friday. Jesus also asked Sister Faustina to pray at the hour of great mercy. Our Lord told her: "At

St. Michael's Church (Vilnius)

three o'clock, implore My mercy, especially for sinners; and, if only for a brief moment, immerse yourself in My Passion, particularly in My abandonment at the moment of agony. This is the hour of great mercy for the whole world. I will allow you to enter into My mortal sorrow. In this hour, I will refuse nothing to the soul that makes a request of Me in virtue of My Passion" (*Diary,* 1320).

In November 1936 when Sister Faustina was ill, she recorded the following vision of heaven:

> Today, I was in heaven, in spirit, and I saw its inconceivable beauties and the happiness that awaits us after death. I saw how all creatures give ceaseless praise and glory to God. I saw how great is happiness in God, which spreads to all creatures, making them happy; and then all the glory and praise which springs from this happiness returns to its source; and they enter into the depths of God, contemplating the inner life of God, the Father, the Son, and the Holy Spirit....
>
> And God has given me to understand that there is but one thing that is of infinite value in His eyes, and that is love of God, love, love and once again, love; and nothing can compare with a single act of pure love of God (*Diary,* 777, 778).

The Visionary after the Apparition

Sister Faustina suffered greatly from various trials, including tuberculosis and misunderstandings from the other sisters. She united her sufferings to those of Jesus and offered them for others, especially for the conversion of persons most in need of God's mercy. Sister Faustina stated that Holy Communion sustained her in her sufferings.

She was an apostle of Divine Mercy until the end of her life. Jesus told her: "I am giving you three ways of exercising mercy toward your neighbor: the first—by deed, the second—by word, the third—by prayer. In these three degrees is contained the fullness of mercy, and it is an unquestionable proof of love for Me" (*Diary*, 742).

Sister Faustina entered a sanatorium in Pradnik, near Krakow, in December 1936. Her tuberculosis worsened and it became more difficult to eat. Pain wracked her body for much of her last year. She left the sanatorium in September 1938 and returned to her convent in Krakow, where she died on October 5, at the age of thirty-three. She was buried in the community's cemetery plot in Lagiewniki, near Krakow. In 1966 her body was transferred to the sisters' chapel in Lagiewniki, under the marble floor at the right side of the chapel. Before her beatification in 1993, the remains were transferred to a reliquary-coffin and placed on the altar beneath the image of the merciful Jesus.

Sister Faustina's tomb (Wronia Street, Krakow)

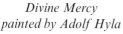

Divine Mercy
painted by Adolf Hyla

Divine Mercy
painted by Stanley Batowski

The Recognition Process

The Divine Mercy devotion in the forms Sister Faustina transmitted began to develop dynamically during the Second World War, and with it grew knowledge of Sister Faustina's holiness. In 1943, her spiritual director and confessor at Krakow, Fr. J. Andrasz, blessed an image of the merciful Jesus painted by Adolf Hyla according to Sister Faustina's vision.

Throughout the war, solemn Divine Mercy services were held that attracted people from Lagiewniki and also from Krakow and its surroundings. The sisters' chapel became a place of public cult. In 1944, Fr. Andrasz blessed a second smaller image of the Merciful Jesus painted by Adolf Hyla that was placed on the lateral altar. This became one of the most popular paintings depicting Our Lord's mercy.

In 1943 another artist, Stanley Batowski, painted an image of the Divine Mercy. This is in Krakow at the Church of Divine Mercy on Smolensk Street. In the 1950s, two more Polish artists completed paintings of the Merciful Jesus—Slendzinski in 1954 and Adam Styka in 1957.

Following the war, the convent in Lagiewniki became the center for the Divine Mercy devotion. Pilgrims came to the convent for spiritual renewal. There, special devotions to the Divine Mercy were held every third Sunday of the month, and the Feast of Divine Mercy was celebrated on the Sunday after Easter. Bishops in various dioceses of Poland granted permission to publish holy cards and prayers to the Divine Mercy. In 1951, Cardinal A. Sapieha granted a plenary indulgence for those who visited the shrine on the Sunday after Easter.

Altar in the Divine Mercy Shrine (Wronia Street, Krakow)

Since the sixties, the chapel with Sister Faustina's crypt and the famous image of the Merciful Jesus was inscribed in the list of pilgrimage places of the Archdiocese of Krakow. In November 1993 Franciszek Cardinal Macharski issued a decree elevating the chapel to the rank of a shrine.

Fr. Joseph Jarzebowski, a Polish Marian priest, brought the Divine Mercy devotion to the United States in 1941. The National Shrine of Divine Mercy was established in Stockbridge, Massachusetts (south of Pittsfield near the New York State border) in 1944.

After the war soldiers and refugees spread this devotion throughout the world, and active centers were established in France, the United States and Australia.

In 1959, the Vatican prohibited the spread of the Divine Mercy devotion in the forms proposed by Sister Faustina due to confusing translations of her diary. Bishops were to decide whether churches in their dioceses should remove the images of the Divine Mercy. But by April 1978, the Holy See had examined previously unavailable documents, reversed its 1959 decision and allowed the spread of the Divine Mercy devotion.

Church of Divine Mercy on Smolensk Street (Krakow)

Archbishop Karol Wojtyla of Krakow (now Pope John Paul II) became the promoter for Sister Faustina's cause of beatification. In October 1965, Archbishop Wojtyla designated Bishop Julian Grobicki to initiate the informative process on the life and virtues of Sister Faustina, who consequently received the title "Servant of God."

The first major step toward sainthood was taken when the Vatican's Congregation for the Causes of Saints acknowledged that Sister Faustina had practiced heroic virtue. On March 7, 1992, she received the title "Venerable Servant of God." On December 21, 1992, the Holy Father published the Church's acceptance of a miracle attributed to the intercession of Sister Faustina, opening the way for her beatification. This took place at St. Peter's Square in Rome on April 18, 1993, the Sunday after Easter—the Feast of Mercy. The approval of another miracle due to her intercession led to her canonization during the Jubilee year in 2000.

In January 1995, in response to the unanimous request of the Polish bishops, the Holy See granted permission to celebrate Mercy Sunday in Poland. In that same year, Pope John Paul II celebrated Mercy Sunday at the Church of the Holy Spirit in Rome.

On March 6, 1996, the Metropolitan of Krakow, Franciszek Cardinal Macharski, initiated at the shrine in Krakow-Lagiewniki an Association of the Apostles of Divine Mercy Faustinum. Its purpose is to help realize the mission of St. Faustina under the direction of the Sisters of Our Lady of Mercy. The main task of the Faustinum is the formation of the Apostles of Divine Mercy.

The Shrine

Thousands of pilgrims from Poland and all over the world visit the shrine in Krakow. The greatest crowds of pilgrims flock there on the Feast of Divine Mercy. The spread of the Divine Mercy devotion has brought more and more pilgrims to the shrine, so a new basilica of Divine Mercy is planned in that area. It will have a ministry for pilgrims and for the apostolic movement of Divine Mercy.

The figure and mission of St. Faustina is close to the Holy Father, as he has expressed on several occasions. He has said that the shrine in Krakow-Lagiewniki is the "capital

Main entrance to the Shrine of Divine Mercy in Krakow-Lagiewniki

of the cult of Divine Mercy." He visited it on June 7, 1997, to pray before the miraculous image of the Merciful Jesus and Blessed Faustina's relics. He said then:

> From here, came out the message of the Divine Mercy that Christ himself chose to pass on to our generation through Blessed Faustina. And it is a message clear and understandable for every-

Plaque commemorating Pope
John Paul II's 1997 visit to the shrine

one. Anyone can come here, look at the image of the Merciful Christ, his heart radiating grace, and hear in the depths of his own soul what Blessed Faustina heard. "Fear nothing, I am with you." And if this person responds with a sincere heart: "Jesus, I trust in you!" he will find comfort in all his anxieties and fears.

Planning a Pilgrimage

Most international pilgrims will probably arrive in Warsaw. It is convenient to stay in a hotel by the train station (such as the Holiday Inn or Marriott) to catch a train to Krakow. Express buses also depart for Lodz from a stop between the station and the

Outdoor chapel on the shrine grounds

Holiday Inn. Besides visiting the Convent of the Sisters of Our Lady of Mercy at 3/9 Zyntia Street in Warsaw, the pilgrim could also visit St. Jakok's church in Ochota, Warsaw, just a short taxi ride from the train station. The Old Town area of Warsaw is a fascinating place to visit. Reconstructed after World War II in a 17th and 18th century style, the Old Town is one of the world's cultural heritage sites. The 15th century St. John's Cathedral is found there. During the Second World War the cathedral was razed, but it has now been reconstructed in its Gothic style.

Convent chapel at 3/9 Zyntia Street (Warsaw)

To visit St. Faustina's birthplace in Glogowiec and St. Casimir's Church in nearby Swinice, the pilgrim can take one of the frequent daily buses from Warsaw to Lodz. The trip lasts less than two hours. In Lodz, an industrial city with a population of close to one million, the pilgrim can visit the Cathedral of St. Stanislaus Kostka and then hire a taxi for a half day to visit Glogowiec and Swinice.

Excellent inter-city express trains from Warsaw to Krakow make the trip in two to three hours. In Krakow, the pilgrim can visit Sister Faustina's convent at 3/9 Wronia Street, now renamed Blessed Faustina Street. The chapel displays the famous painting of Divine Mercy by Adolf Hyla. While in Krakow the pilgrim could also visit the Franciscan church on Smolensk Street to see Stanley Batowski's painting of the merciful Jesus. The beautiful city of

Krakow, with a population of about one million, stayed intact during the war and preserves its medieval architecture. The main market square in the Old Town is the largest medieval square in Poland. St. Mary's Church overlooks the square.

The pilgrim may wish to visit Vilnius, the capital of Lithuania, where Sister Faustina lived for some time. Daily flights from Warsaw to Vilnius take less than an hour. A picturesque city, Vilnius is extremely clean and reminds one of Switzerland. Although it has only a few hotels from the international chains (such as Radisson), there are many smaller ones of quite good standards. If one stays in or near the Old Town, one can walk to the *Ostra Brama* (East Gate) that has a painting of Our Lady of Mercy easily viewed from the street below. Since the 16th century, the Dawn or East Gate was the site of veneration of an icon of the Blessed Virgin's Annunciation. It is also easy to walk to the Church of the Holy Spirit on Dominican Street, where one can view Eugene Kazimierowski's painting of the image of Divine Mercy.

In the Old Town, one can visit St. Michael's Church, now a museum of architecture. A taxi can bring the pilgrim to the convent at 29 Grybo Street where Sister Faustina spent part of her life. Cathedral Square lies on the outskirts of the Old Town. The cathedral was converted to a picture gallery during the Soviet era but was reconsecrated in 1989, and Mass is celebrated daily. The cathedral has a chapel dedicated to St. Kazimieras, the country's patron saint.

Should time permit, the pilgrim may wish to visit Siauliai, a small city north of Kaunas, a few hours from Vilnius. Siauliai is famous for its Hill of Crosses. Thousands of crosses have been planted on this site of national pilgrimage since the 14th century.

CHAPTER TEN

The Virgin of the Golden Heart

BEAURAING, BELGIUM (1932–1933)

Apparition site at Beauraing

Summary

In Beauraing, Belgium, the Blessed Virgin appeared thirty-three times between November 1932 and January 1933 to four girls and a boy. Our Lady told the children she was the Immaculate Virgin. She asked for prayer and sacrifice and promised to bring people to conversion. She is known as the Virgin of the Golden Heart because the children saw a golden heart surrounded by glittering rays during her later appearances.

The Historical Context

The great depression had struck Europe in the early 1930s. Mussolini ruled Italy. Hitler's Nazism would soon control Germany, and communism dominated Russia. Religious turmoil accompanied this political upheaval as European Catholics increasingly drifted away from the Church and its sacraments.

Beauraing, an agricultural village of two thousand people in the Walloon or French-speaking area of Belgium, lies sixty miles southeast of Brussels and twelve miles from Dinant. Only a few miles from the French border, Beauraing is sixty miles from Reims, famous for its Gothic cathedral.

The Apparition

Thirteen-year-old Gilberte Voisin attended a school staffed by the Sisters of Christian Doctrine in Beauraing. Her father, Hector Voisin, was a railway worker who had strayed from the Church.

Village of Beauraing

Her mother ran a small store selling wallpaper and paint. Hector sent his daughter Fernande, fifteen, and son Albert, eleven, to meet and walk Gilberte home each day after school.

The two children walked to the school to meet their sister around 6:00 P.M. on the cold, windy night of November 29, 1932. As they passed the Degeimbre house, another two girls joined them, Andrée and Gilberte Degeimbre, fourteen and nine respectively.

As the children rang the convent doorbell for Gilberte Voisin, Albert looked toward a high railroad viaduct over the street about fifty yards away. Amazement spread over his face. The Blessed Virgin, dressed in a white gown and a white veil falling to her shoulders, was walking in the air over the viaduct and a Lourdes grotto in the convent yard. Rays surrounded her head, forming a crown of sunshine. Blue light shimmered from her left shoulder to her right foot. Albert shouted to his companions, who also saw the luminous Virgin Mary walking through the air. A small cloud, perhaps symbolic of heaven, covered her feet.

Sister Valeria came to the convent door and called Gilberte. The girl saw the Blessed Virgin immediately, but the Sister saw nothing and sent the children home. The children's parents didn't believe the story either.

The railway viaduct

The five children again saw the Lady above the viaduct as they walked home from school the next day. They ran to get Mrs. Degeimbre, but she saw nothing. The following evening, December 1, the Lady appeared again. She rose toward heaven from the shrubs near the Lourdes grotto in the convent yard, and vanished. Later she appeared by a hawthorn tree in the garden. She looked about eighteen to twenty years old and wore a long, white pleated gown with no belt. The dress seemed to radiate a blue light. The Blessed Virgin held her hands together in prayer, then disappeared.

The next evening, December 2, Albert asked the Lady if she was the Immaculate Virgin,[3] and she nodded

Painting of Mary and the children of Beauraing

yes. Albert then asked what she wanted of them. She replied, "Always be good," and then left. Meanwhile, word had spread and crowds began to gather each evening as the apparitions continued. When the Blessed Mother appeared on December 6, she held a shining rosary.

The children arrived on December 8, the feast of the Immaculate Conception, along with a crowd of about fifteen thousand, who were hoping to see something miraculous. The children entered a state of complete ecstasy, oblivious to the crowd. They

---

3. The term "Immaculate Conception" means Mary was conceived free of original sin and endowed with grace. The term "Immaculate Virgin" means she remained sinless for her entire life.

fell to the ground simultaneously and knelt, their eyes focused on the same point in space. Their faces radiated happiness.

Some doctors had come to examine the children during the apparition. Dr. Lurquin placed a burning match under Gilberte Voisin's left hand but the child, in a trance, noticed nothing. Gilberte suffered neither burns nor pain afterward. Other doctors pinched and pricked the five children and directed high-powered flashlights into their eyes. They did not react.

After that, the Virgin Mary did not come every evening. On December 17 she asked that a chapel be built at Beauraing. Four days later, on December 21, she told the children she was the Immaculate Virgin. On December 23, when asked why she came, Mary replied, "So people will come here on pilgrimage."

A crowd of about eight thousand gathered at the convent grounds on December 29. That night Mary showed the children a vision of her Immaculate Heart. Fernande saw a golden heart in the Virgin's chest with glittering rays shining out from it. Mary opened her arms to the children. After that, the Immaculate Heart of Mary became a distinctive feature of the Beauraing apparitions. The following day, on December 30, Andrée Degeimbre and Fernande and Gilberte Voisin saw the golden heart of Mary.

Mary, Virgin of the Golden Heart, surrounded by votive candles

The stone chapel built at Mary's request

The apparition remained silent during her appearance on December 31, but all the children saw her golden heart. It differed from the Pietà in the small chapel nearby that showed Mary's sorrowful heart as she held the crucified Jesus in her hands. Here, Mary's heart radiated love and light for all her children.

"Pray. Pray very much," Our Lady told Gilberte Voisin on January 1, 1933. The next day, she said she would speak to each of the children separately. The apparitions were coming to their close.

From thirty thousand to thirty-five thousand people gathered at the convent during the last Beauraing apparition on January 3, 1933. Our Lady first revealed individual secrets to four of the five children (excluding Fernande), showing her special attention to each one. Deeply touched, tears ran down the children's faces. "I will convert sinners," Mary promised. "I am the Mother of God, the Queen of Heaven. Pray all the time."

As Fernande knelt after the other children had gone to be questioned in the convent, she heard a clap of thunder and saw a brilliant light on the hawthorn bush, like flames of fire. The Blessed Virgin then appeared, asking, "Do you love my Son? Do you love me? Then sacrifice yourself for me. Good-bye." Before Our Lady disappeared, the child had a marvelous vision of the Immaculate Heart of Mary, shining with light and love.

Statue of Mary, Virgin of the Golden Heart

Two million people visited the sanctuary of Beauraing that year. Both Mr. and Mrs. Voisin soon returned to the sacraments and the practice of the Catholic faith.

At Beauraing, Mary gave a message of hope for the world. Asking for prayer and sacrifice, she promised to intercede for the faithful, and said she would bring the sinful to convert and reconcile with God.

The Visionaries after the Apparition

All the children remained devoted Catholics for their entire lives. They have avoided the limelight, saying they were merely the instruments through whom Mary gave her message to the world. After World War II, Albert married and taught in mission schools in the Belgian Congo. He returned to Beauraing in 1961. Each of the girls married and raised families. Andrée died in 1978, Fernande in 1979.

Miraculous Cures

Maria Van Laer, thirty-three, had been an invalid for sixteen years, suffering from tuberculosis. She also had a deformed spinal column and large tumors that had developed into open sores. All her tumors and sores disappeared instantly on her second visit to the Beauraing sanctuary in 1933.

Pauline Dereppe, ten, had a bone disease with painful sores. On December 4 Albert had asked the Virgin to heal Pauline, and the Lady simply smiled. On February 15, after praying at the apparition site, Pauline was cured.

The spring at Beauraing

The Recognition Process

In 1935 the bishop of Namur, whose diocese includes Beauraing, set up a commission to examine the events. On February 2, 1943, the bishop approved devotions to Our Lady of Beauraing. On August 22, 1946, he blessed a large marble statue of Our Lady of Beauraing, placed under the hawthorn where Mary appeared to the children.

On the Feast of the Immaculate Heart in 1947, work was begun on the chapel that Our Lady had requested. Bishop Charue of Namur granted final approbation on July 2, 1949.

"Most holy God, you chose Mary, the Immaculate Virgin, as Mother of your Word made flesh," the bishop prayed at the Mass honoring Our Lady of Beauraing. "Deign to convert our hearts when we recognize our sin before you and enable us to love your Son more and more. We ask this through Jesus Christ, our Lord and our God, who reigns with you in the unity of the Holy Spirit, forever and ever. Amen."

Pope John Paul II visited the Beauraing sanctuary on May 18, 1985.

The Shrine

A wooded park with a 16th century feudal castle formerly belonging to the Dukes of Ossuna, now known as the *Domaine Marial,* was acquired on January 14, 1946. There, less than a mile from the apparition site, the pilgrim can follow the Way of the Cross.

The Votive Chapel has a chapel of perpetual adoration and three confessionals. One side of the chapel has five windows, each sixteen feet high, symbolizing the five children who saw Our Lady. To the right is a single window for Mary. The thirty-three stones in the arch outside the chapel symbolize the thirty-three apparitions of Our Lady in Beauraing.

Opened on May 1, 1951, the Marian museum has a collection of eight hundred Marian statues from around the world. The sanctuary was dedicated on August 21, 1954. Both the guest house *(Hospitalité)* and the Reception House *(Accueil)* opened on May 1, 1956. The opening ceremony for the *Crypte St. Jean* took place on November 29, 1961, and the altar of the garden was consecrated on May 3, 1962. A modern new basilica known as the Upper Church was opened

Mosaics of the crowning of Mary (above) and Pentecost (below) by Max Van der Linden

Tapestry at the entrance to the Upper Church

on October 6, 1968. A youth hostel called the House of Epi opened in the *Domaine Marial* on November 29, 1980.

A large esplanade leads to the Upper Church. Inside, artwork includes a ceramic Way of the Cross, made by Max Van der Linden. The church also has a painting by the Parisian artist, Maurice Rocher, depicting Mary, Mother of God, holding the infant Jesus.

Bronze railings surround the red flowering hawthorn tree and the garden sanctuary. The rosary is recited daily at 6:30 P.M. at the marble statue by the hawthorn tree, sculpted by A. Pierroux. Candles constantly burn on the gigantic votive candlestand. An open-air altar stands on the spot where the Lourdes grotto had been. On the wall of the garden, an inscription with letters engraved in gold states: "Here under the hawthorn during the last of her apparitions, the Virgin Mary showed her Immaculate Heart."

About one million pilgrims annually visit the shrine. In Beauraing, August 22 is celebrated as the Feast of the Immaculate Heart of Mary, the official Beauraing feast and the time of a great international pilgrimage. The anniversary of the apparitions is celebrated on November 29.

The sanctuary has an official bulletin, the bi-monthly *La Voix de Beauraing.*

In Lowell, Massachusetts, the *Pro Maria* Committee is dedicated to spreading the message of Beauraing in the United States.

Planning a Pilgrimage

Rail service is convenient between Brussels and Beauraing via Dinant. From the citadel of Dinant, one has a splendid panoramic view of the valley of the Meuse. The impressive Church of Our Lady *(Collégiale Notre-Dame)* in Dinant is topped by a bell tower in the shape of a bulb. Dinant also has an interesting underground cave called the *Merveilleuse.*

Other towns in the Belgium province of Namur also hold tourist attractions. The pilgrim can visit Chevetogne, home of the largest Byzantine church built in a non-Orthodox country.

Church of Our Lady in Dinant, Belgium

La Grande Place in Brussels

Andenne has the oldest Romanesque church in Belgium. Floreffe's abbey was founded on a rocky spur in 1121. Both Maredesous and Maredret have Benedictine abbeys. The Cathedral of St. Auban is located in Namur, the provincial capital.

While in Brussels, capital of the Kingdom of Belgium since 1830, the pilgrim could visit the Gothic Cathedral of St. Michael and *La Grande Place,* a beautiful market square surrounded by 17th-century guild buildings. Brussels is also the administrative home for the Commission of the European Communities.

West by train, the pilgrim can visit the historic town of Brugge, often called the Venice of the North because of its many canals. In the Church of Notre Dame, the pilgrim can see Michelangelo's Virgin and Child, one of his few paintings to be found outside Italy. Further west of Brugge, the seaside resort of Ostend is an important link for maritime traffic with England.

The lovely city of Louvain, famous for its university founded in 1425 and the Gothic Church of St. Peter, lies slightly east of Brussels.

The Town Hall of the city of Antwerp, found in Belgium's northernmost province, is a masterpiece of Flemish Renaissance architecture. The Cathedral of Our Lady is the largest gothic church in the region.

Pilgrims may also wish to cross the French border and visit Reims, once an important city of Roman Gaul. It is less than sixty miles from Beauraing. Charles II's coronation, in the presence of Joan of Arc, was held in Reims. The Cathedral of Notre Dame, began in 1211 on the site of an old Romanesque church, is a Gothic masterpiece. Above the central portal are stone sculptures of scenes in the Virgin Mary's life including the annunciation, the visitation and her coronation in heaven. The Cathedral in Reims is also called the Cathedral of Angels because of its many statues of angels.

CHAPTER ELEVEN

The Virgin of the Poor

Banneux, Belgium (1933)

Mariette Beco and Our Lady at Banneux

Summary

The Virgin Mary appeared eight times to Mariette Beco near the village of Banneux, Belgium, from January to March 1933. "I am the Virgin of the Poor," Our Lady told the girl. Mary asked for a small chapel and called people to prayer. She invited Mariette to come to the spring, symbolic of Christ as the source and fountain of all grace and salvation.

Banneux street with hotels, restaurants and shops

The Historical Context

Banneux is on a one thousand foot plateau surrounded by pine forests, on the Pepinster-Verviers route in eastern Belgium. It lies slightly northwest of the popular health resort of Spa, twelve miles southeast of Liège and fifty miles east of Beauraing. It is near the borders of Germany, the Netherlands and Luxembourg. The name "Banneux" derives from the word *banalitér,* a term referring to the right of the poor to have partial use of the surrounding forests.

The villagers vowed in 1914 to consecrate their town to Our Lady if it escaped the ravages of war. Banneux was unharmed during World War I and the village was thereafter called "Banneux Notre Dame."

Banneux had only 325 inhabitants when Mariette Beco was born on March 25, 1921, the feast of the Annunciation. She was the eldest of seven children. In the 1930s, Belgium was suffering from the world depression. Julien Beco, Mariette's father, was an unemployed wiremaker whose only income came from farming a garden in his front yard. He had drifted away from the Church years before. The family lived in a small brick house Mariette's father had built, half a mile outside the village, facing a pine forest.

The Apparition

Mariette Beco, age eleven, first encountered the Virgin Mary on the cold wintry night of Sunday, January 15, 1933, twelve days after the apparitions in Beauraing had ended. The girl looked out the window at 7:00 P.M. and saw a radiant young woman in the front yard of the Beco home.

The woman looked like an image of light. She wore a dazzling white gown with a blue sash at the waist, and a transparent white veil covered her head and shoulders. A golden rose could be seen on her right foot, slightly exposed. Her right hand held a rosary of diamond-like brilliancy. She seemed suspended on a small cloud a foot and a half above the ground.

"Mother! A woman is in our yard," Mariette shouted, but her mother ignored her story. The Lady beckoned the girl to come out but Mariette's mother stopped her at the front door. The mysterious visitor had disappeared when Mariette returned to the window.

Painting of the apparition at Banneux

The next day at school, Mariette told the story to her friend Josephine Léonard, who then told Fr. Jamin, the young parish priest. He dismissed the story, thinking Mariette must have heard about the Beauraing apparitions. Mariette, however, now began to faithfully attend morning Mass and catechism class. Since she had been absent for the past several months, this astonished the priest.

Our Lady's statue by the fountain

Three days later, Wednesday, January 18, Mariette saw the luminous Virgin Mary descend from between the tops of two tall pine trees at 7:00 P.M. Mariette got up and walked into the garden despite the intense cold. The Virgin came to rest about fifteen inches above the ground five feet in front of Mariette. The white rosary once again hung from Our Lady's right forearm. She beckoned, and Mariette followed the gliding apparition down the road.

Mariette's father followed and saw his daughter praying in a state of ecstasy. He got on his bicycle to fetch Fr. Jamin, but the priest was still away at Liège. Julien Beco then returned home with a neighbor, Michael Charlesèche, and his son Louis. The three observers heard Mariette repeat the words of Our Lady but did not see the apparition.

Suddenly, Mariette dropped to her knees in the snow by a ditch. "Put your hands in the water," the Blessed Virgin said. Mariette followed the instructions. "This stream is reserved for me," Our Lady said, then disappeared. The apparition had lasted almost an hour.

Fr. Louis Jamin returned home later Wednesday evening and heard the story. He visited the Beco home, but Mariette was asleep. As he was leaving, Mariette's father asked to meet the priest the next day to return to the sacraments. This surprised Fr. Jamin because he had earlier prayed for a sign—such as the conversion of Mariette's father—to confirm the reality of the apparitions of Beauraing.

At 7:00 P.M. on Thursday, January 19, Mariette and her father entered the garden, where eleven other people had gathered. Mariette knelt in the snow and began to pray. After reciting several decades of the rosary, she saw the apparition. "Who are you?" Mariette asked the Lady. "I am the Virgin of the Poor," she responded. Mariette returned to the spring, and Our Lady said, "This spring is reserved for all nations—to relieve the sick." This apparition was much shorter than the others, lasting about seven minutes. Mariette returned home with her father. During questioning, it became clear she did not know the meaning of the word "nations."

Mariette saw the Blessed Virgin again in the front yard on Friday, January 20. "What do you want?" Mariette asked. "A small

"This spring is reserved for all nations—to relieve the sick."

chapel," Mary replied. The Virgin blessed Mariette with the sign of the cross, and the girl fainted. The Becos summoned Dr. Chaumont, who examined Mariette and found her pulse beating normally.

Every evening Mariette went to the garden and prayed the rosary, but the apparitions had stopped. The Virgin did not appear for three more weeks. Mariette's classmates taunted her in catechism class during that time, calling her Bernadette and asking for her blessing. Some even struck her in the face.

The Blessed Virgin appeared to Mariette again on Saturday evening, February 11, the feast of Our Lady of Lourdes. Mariette was praying the rosary when she saw the Blessed Virgin in the gar-

The chapel requested by Our Lady

den as during the previous times. "I come to relieve suffering," Mary said.

During the sixth apparition, on Wednesday, February 15, Mariette asked Mary for a sign. The parish priest had told the girl to make this request. Our Lady replied simply, "Believe in me; I will believe in you. Pray much." She confided a secret Mariette never revealed. The apparition lasted only ten minutes.

The seventh apparition occurred on February 20. Smiling, the Blessed Virgin led Mariette to the spring. There she told her, "My dear child, pray much." Then she stopped smiling.

Rain soaked Mariette as she recited the rosary in the yard two weeks later, on Thursday, March 2. The downpour stopped and she saw the Blessed Virgin for the eighth and final time. Our Lady appeared sad. "I am the Mother of the Savior, Mother of God. Pray much," Mary said, then blessed Mariette as she had in the fourth apparition. Mary then bid farewell to Mariette: "Adieu—until we meet in God." Then the Virgin disappeared over the pine trees.

Unlike other apparitions of Our Lady, those in Banneux never drew large crowds. Less than twenty people came when Mariette prayed in the garden each evening.

The Visionary after the Apparition

Mariette married and raised a family. She avoided all publicity, seeing herself as a mere instrument of Our Lady, not a public attraction. She remained a firm proponent of the message of Our Lady.

Louis Jamin, the priest, died on March 2, 1961 and Msgr. Kerkhofs, the bishop who approved the Banneux apparitions, died on December 31, 1962.

Miraculous Cures

Bishop Kerkhofs documented twenty miraculous cures from 1933 through 1938. Mrs. Goethals of Anvers, Belgium, had suffered deafness, constant pain and fractured bones resulting from a car accident. She could eat no solid food. After drinking from the spring at

Stone monument in honor of Bishop Kerkhofs

*Votive candles burn
continuously at the shrine*

Banneux, Mrs. Goethals' pain disappeared, she regained her hearing, and she could eat solid food again.

Laura Pletinck, twenty, suffered from cerebrospinal meningitis. She had been bedridden for seven years, both legs paralyzed, when she went on pilgrimage to Banneux. Free of pain, Laura could walk the next day.

The first pilgrimages of invalids took place from Paris (1954), Ireland and England (1956), and Italy (1972).

Wall with spigots for water from the fountain

The Recognition Process

In 1935 the Bishop of Liège appointed a commission to investigate the Banneux events. World War II interrupted the work. The Ardennes region suffered bitter fighting at the Battle of the Bulge, late in the war.

Finally, on August 22, 1949, Bishop Kerkhofs of Liège issued a pastoral letter affirming Mariette Beco's claims as worthy of belief. He wrote: "Twice, first in 1942 and then in 1947, we have officially recognized, with certain reservations, the reality of the apparitions at Banneux. Today, after further years of prayer and careful investigation, we believe that we can and must recognize without reservation the reality of the eight apparitions of the Blessed Virgin to Mariette Beco."

Pope John Paul II visited the Banneux sanctuary on May 21, 1985.

The Shrine

Fr. Jamin drew the sketches for the little stone chapel and the esplanade. The first chapel stone was laid on May 25, 1933, and the completed chapel was blessed on the Assumption, August 15, 1933. The first Mass was celebrated on September 8, the liturgical feast of Mary's birth. The chapel itself is small—twenty-four feet wide and thirty-four feet to the top of the belfry. It is built over the spot in the garden where Our Lady appeared. A white slab marks this spot, bearing the words *Huc veniens volvit matris recludere pectus* (Coming here, she wanted to open her mother's heart).

The Little Chapel

The chapel contains an altar and tabernacle, as well as a painting of the apparition scene done by Léon Jamin, Fr. Louis Jamin's

Stained glass window in the Little Chapel

uncle. The inside walls of the chapel hold over 1,500 plaques testifying to the many favors received from Our Lady at Banneux. The esplanade was inaugurated on August 15, 1939.

On the path from the Little Chapel to the spring three round stone slabs indicate where Mariette knelt and prayed when Mary beckoned her to come to the spring, symbolic of Christ. Near the spring a large basin with the words, *Poussez vos mains dans l'eau,* invites the pilgrims to put their hands in the water.

A cloister with the statue of St. Louis Grignion de Montfort, who promoted devotion to Mary, is opposite the altar at the spring.

Over five hundred thousand pilgrims annually visit the Banneux sanctuary. The rosary has been recited nightly at 7:00 P.M. since 1933, even during World War II. An open chapel stands at the spot where the Blessed Virgin appeared at the spring. Pilgrims can quench their thirst with spring water from several outlets in a wall. A hospitality center for the sick was built in 1938 opposite the Little Chapel and is staffed by the Sisters of St. Vincent de Paul of Gijzegem. It was then enlarged in 1954 to hold two hundred sick and handicapped pilgrims. A new facility opened in 1993 can accommodate 240 pilgrims in comfortable twin bedded rooms.

The Chapel of the Message is on one side of the esplanade. In front of the chapel stands a colonnade with seven arches. Two frescoes appear on either side of the altar—one depicts the small vegetable garden and the Beco house, and the other depicts the spring on the side of the country road. To the left of the altar is an entrance to the small Chapel of Mary Mediatrix. Two large frescoes depict the annunciation of the angel and Mary's visit to Elizabeth. The fresco on the back wall depicts the Virgin of the Poor as she appeared to Mariette, leading her to the spring.

The Chapel of the Sick on the other side of the esplanade also has a colonnade of arches. Here the celebration of the Eucharist is held for the sick. Behind the altar is a picture of the Virgin of the Poor, and also a bas-relief of St. Francis of Assisi.

Above the main altar in the esplanade appear the words *Mère du Sauveur, Mère de Dieu* (Mother of the Savior, Mother of God).

The Way of the Cross begins in the woods by the chapel dedicated to St. Michael, the patron of Germany. Stained glass windows depict sixteen stations of the cross (two more than usual). The first shows the Last Supper, and the last one is the resurrection of Our Lord.

Taking the Avenue of the Magnificat, the pilgrim passes the shrine of St. Bernadette and the Chapel of St. Thérèse.

A chalet for youth was constructed in 1982. A new Pilgrim's Church was dedicated on May 1, 1984. A house for the priests called the Abri du Curé d'Ars is found behind the Little Chapel.

*Statue of the Virgin of the Poor outside
the Open Air Chapel (behind the fountain)*

The Sanctuary publishes a bi-monthly magazine entitled *La Vierge des Pauvres.*

Planning a Pilgrimage

Nestled in the peaceful surroundings of the Ardennes region, the sanctuary is easily accessible to pilgrims from Belgium, the Netherlands and Germany. The regular train service from Brussels to Liège takes about an hour. The Brussels-Liège-Verviers train service takes an hour and a half. From Liège and Verviers, one can take a bus to Banneux. Liège is only thirty minutes by train from Maastricht in the Netherlands.

In Liège, the pilgrim could visit the Town Hall, built in 1714.

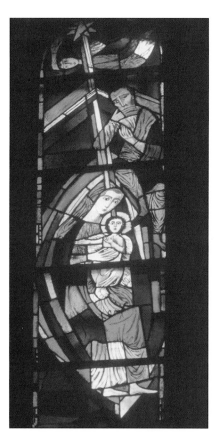

Shrine of Our Lady of the Sea in Maastricht

For a panoramic view of the city, climb the 407 steps of the *Montagne de Buerren,* leading to the Citadel.

In the town of Huy on the Meuse River, the pilgrim could visit the beautiful Church of Our Lady, or *Collégiale Notre-Dame.*

The town of Spa, famous for its springs and called the "Pearl of the Ardennes," lies southeast of Banneux. There one can see the neo-Romanesque Church of St. Remacle. In Malmedy, slightly south of Spa, a cathedral dating from 1775 is consecrated jointly to Saints Peter, Paul and Quirin. Further south but still in Liège Province is Stavelot, where St. Remacle founded an abbey in 648.

If pilgrims visit nearby Maastricht, in the Netherlands, they could see the popular Marian sanctuary Our Lady of the Sea. Slightly north of Maastricht, another important Marian shrine is found in the city of s'Herto-genbosch.

Pilgrims may also wish to cross the German border and visit the old Roman city of Aachen, north of Banneux. Charlemagne built the octagonal Cathedral of Aachen from 786 to 800. Between 946 and 1531 thirty German kings and emperors had their coronation in the cathedral. The cathedral's treasury contains the Shrine of the Virgin Mary, a small silver reproduction of a church dating from 1220. The Virgin Mary, with Jesus on her lap, is enthroned at the entrance of this sculpture.

CHAPTER TWELVE

Our Lady, Mother of All People

ZEITOUN, CAIRO, EGYPT (1968)

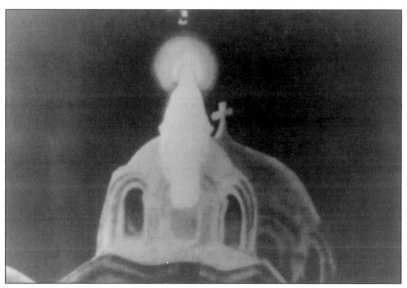

The aura of the Virgin Mary on the roof of St. Mary's Coptic Church

Summary

From 1968 to 1971 the Virgin Mary appeared at a church in Zeitoun, a suburb of Cairo. Throngs of Christians and Muslims sang and prayed in Coptic, Arabic and Greek, while luminous doves, lights and fragrant clouds at times accompanied the appearances. Sometimes smiling, at other times the Virgin looked serious, even sad.

As at Knock, Mary remained silent during these visions. As the Mother of all people, she came to open humanity to God's redeeming grace. More than a million people viewed her, and a number of miraculous cures followed. In 1968 the bishop of the Coptic Orthodox Church approved the apparitions as worthy of belief.

The Historical Context

The Islamic faith dominates Egypt, but about six percent of the people are Christian, mostly Coptic Orthodox. Approximately 180,000 Copts are united to Rome.

The old cathedral

In the early days of Christianity, a number of sees—centers of authority or jurisdiction—were established as residential cities of bishops, including Antioch in Syria, Alexandria in Egypt, and Rome in Italy. According to a tradition based on the Ecclesiastical History of Eusebius (late third century), St. Mark founded the See of Alexandria when he came to Egypt to preach Christianity.

The See of Alexandria, the center of the Coptic Orthodox Church, separated from the other churches because of doctrinal differences after the Council of Chalcedon in 451. The Patriarch of Alexandria became known as the "Coptic Pope," a title still used.

Thus, the Coptic Orthodox and Roman Catholic Churches have been separated for fifteen centuries. But relations between them have improved in the last thirty years. For example, in 1968 Pope Paul VI authorized the return of most of St. Mark's relics from Venice to Egypt. In 1973, Pope Paul VI invited the Patriarch of Alexandria to Rome, where they prayed together.

The district of Zeitoun (Arabic for "olives") is about ten miles northeast of Cairo's center. Zeitoun is in the vicinity of ancient Heliopolis, a Greek name meaning "City of the Sun." The Coptic Church of St. Mary, built in 1924, is at the intersection of Tumanbay, Zeitoun's main street, and Khalil Lane.

St. Mary's Church was built after a member of the Khalil Ibrahim family saw the Virgin Mary in a dream in 1918. The Virgin told him to have a Coptic Church built on this site in her honor. He obeyed, and construction was finished in 1924. Fifty years after the dream, Mary graced the church with her appearances.

According to early Christian tradition, the Holy Family passed by this area when they fled from Herod to Egypt. Fourteen shrines commemorate the supposed route of their flight.

Turmoil broke out in the Middle East when Egypt fought a disastrous war with Israel in June 1967. The following year Mary appeared in Egypt.

The Apparition

At 8:30 P.M. on April 2, 1968, a group of Muslim laborers were arriving for the night shift at a garage for Cairo's public transportation system, opposite St. Mary's Church. A movement on the church's middle dome distracted several women pedestrians. Then two of the workmen stared in disbelief at a vision of a "white lady" who knelt at the cross on the dome.

Farouk Mohammed Atwa, one of the workmen, first thought it was a young girl about to jump. "Don't jump!" he shouted, pointing a bandaged finger. Infected with gangrene, his finger was to be amputated the next day. He ran to call the fire brigade while his companions hurried into the church to summon a priest.

The Lady then rose. Luminous, her robes shimmered in the light. "*Settena Mariam,* Our Lady Mary!" shouted a woman below. A flock of glowing white doves suddenly appeared from nowhere to hover above the apparition. Our Lady disappeared a few minutes later, leaving the spectators speechless.

When Farouk Atwa went to the hospital the next day, the surgeon who removed the bandages was astonished to find that the workman's finger had healed completely—the first of many of Our Lady's miraculous healings at Zeitoun.

A series of apparitions, lasting from a few minutes to several hours, began a week later. The priest of the church of St. Mary, Fr. Constantine Moussa, saw

Aura of Mary above the roof of the old church

some of them. At first, Mary appeared almost nightly, usually preceded by mysterious lights flashing like shooting stars or meteorites above the church. Within minutes, as many as twelve luminous doves would fly in formation, occasionally in the form of a cross, close to the church. The doves did not flap their wings but glided, then vanished, followed by a blinding explosion of light.

The light would then shape into the brilliant form of Our Lady wearing a white robe and a bluish-white veil. A dazzling halo shone around her head. Her radiance reminded some Zeitoun citizens of the transfiguration of Jesus with Moses and Elijah on Mount Tabor.

Mary sometimes folded her hands in prayer, and occasionally knelt by the cross on the main church dome as her human form bathed the Church in radiant light. She glided with ease across the domes, bowing to the throngs of spectators below. Our Lady looked like a phosphorous statue, almost fluid, sixteen to twenty feet above the dome. She sometimes appeared above the palm trees in the church courtyard.

White doves accompanied Our Lady

Hundreds watched the Blessed Virgin from 8:00 P.M. to 5:00 A.M. on May 4 and June 8. She occasionally cradled the Infant Jesus in her arms. Other times, St. Joseph and the Christ Child, who seemed about eight years old, appeared with her. She often wore a dazzling crown of light.

The 1968 apparitions generated widespread excitement in Cairo. Catholics, Copts and Muslims all prayed together. Crowds exceeding 250,000 caused tremendous traffic jams. People packed the area so tightly that they had to stand fully erect, arms by their sides, and move with the flow. The crowds grew so large that government authorities closed the street to traffic, demolished the garage, and cut some of the palm trees to prevent accidents. (People were climbing them to better view the apparitions.)

The Virgin Mary acknowledged the salutations from the crowds by bowing, waving her hand, holding a symbolic olive branch, and blessing the people. Billowing red clouds of smoke giving off a fragrance of incense rose around the vision, with no other clouds in the sky.

The apparitions tapered off during the summer, and the crowds at the all-night vigils declined. By late 1968, nightly crowds had diminished to about ten thousand. Mary appeared an average of only once a month by early 1970. That year, especially memorable appearances occurred on the nights of January 6, February 14 and March 6. In October 1970, the street was reopened to traffic. The Blessed Virgin last appeared in Zeitoun on May 29, 1971.

The Virgin never spoke while in Zeitoun. Perhaps this facilitated her acceptance. Copts, Catholics and Muslims alike felt a bond with her, drawn to her personally.

Crowds witnessing Our Lady's appearance in 1968

Fortunately, we have eyewitness reports by Pearl Zaki who documented the events in her book *Our Lord's Mother Visits Egypt in 1968 and 1969*. Francis Johnston (1980) and Michel Nil (1980) have also done research, providing more details on the apparitions. Photographs clearly show the Virgin's luminous form, or aura, with a halo around her head as she stood by the dome of St. Mary's Church.

The Virgin Mary reportedly appeared on the roof of the Church of St. Damiana in Shoubra, another district of Cairo on March 25, 1986. She also is said to have appeared in the 1980s in the Church of St. Mary in Maadi, Egypt and in St. Mary's Church in Edfu in Upper Egypt.

Miraculous Cures

The first miraculous cure at Zeitoun was that of the workman, Farouk Mohammed Atwa, whose gangrenous finger was healed. In addition, Wagih Rizk Matta, who first photographed the apparition in the early hours of April 13, suddenly realized that a serious arm injury he had was completely cured.

The Coptic Orthodox Church established an official medical committee of seven physicians and professors, headed by university medical professor Dr. Shaafik Abdel-Malek, to investigate claimed cures.

Among the more famous miraculous cures was that of forty-year-old Sami Adb-el-Malek, cured of a malignant bladder tumor, the size of a lemon, after visiting Zeitoun.

Fatima Zahi Reda, a devout Muslim housewife in Cairo, suffered from a serious thyroid disease and was too ill to visit Zeitoun. But her husband went, saw Mary's apparition, and prayed for her intercession. He returned home to find his wife miraculously cured.

*Fresco of Mary in
the old cathedral*

Mrs. Mahmoud Shoukry Ibrahim, a forty-five-year-old paralytic, went to Zeitoun in a wheelchair on April 30, 1968, then returned on May 13, the feast of Our Lady of Fatima. She saw a brilliant figure of the Blessed Virgin above the church dome, and prayed for a cure. Suddenly her limbs trembled. She rose from her wheelchair and walked unaided the next morning, astonishing her doctors.

After more than three years of suffering from a severe hernia, Dr. William Nashed Zaki was cured on May 30, after praying to Mary for a cure at Zeitoun.

Medical specialists were unable to cure twenty-year-old Madiha Mohammed Said, a Muslim woman who had lost both her sight and speech. Her brothers took her to the Zeitoun church where she saw the Blessed Virgin on June 28, 1968, and was immediately cured.

The Recognition Process

Pope Kyrillos VI appointed a committee of eminent Coptic clergy-men who submitted their report on May 5, 1968. Committee members spoke with both Muslim and Christian witnesses, and also personally saw both the Blessed Virgin appear on the Church dome to bless the multitudes, and the silver doves radiating light. Kyrillos VI officially pronounced Mary's appearances at the Zeitoun church as credible and worthy of belief.

Our Holy Mother came to Egypt, he believed, because she had found refuge there two thousand years before with Joseph and Jesus. Six Cairo newspapers reported the Patriarch's announcement on May 5, 1968, including the semi-official government paper *Al Ahram*. It was also reported in the *Figaro* of Paris and the *New York Times* on May 5, and the *London Times* on May 6.

"It is no doubt a real appearance, confirmed by many Coptic Catholics of the highest integrity and reliability," announced Cardinal Stephanos I, Patriarch of the Catholic Copts in union with Rome. "This unique miracle embodies a benevolent message that will make the Zeitoun Church a center of pilgrimage." Pope Paul VI made no official pronouncement from Rome because the visions occurred in a Coptic Orthodox church.

The Egyptian government investigated the possibility of fraud and reported they had found no such evidence.

The Shrine

At the entrance to the 1924 church is a larger-than-life painting of the luminous Mary as she appeared to the artist, Sabri Ibrahim, in a crowd that saw the Blessed Virgin in 1968. Entering, one looks up at the dome to see another beautiful painting of the Virgin.

When his Holiness Pope Senouoda III became head of the Coptic Orthodox Church, he approved construction of a new cathedral of the Virgin. More than four thousand people attend Mass in the cathedral each Sunday.

The Coptic Orthodox Church celebrates April 2 as a feast day for Mary in honor of her holy visit to Zeitoun.

The old cathedral of Zeitoun

Entrance to the old cathedral

Mosaic of Our Lady in the ceiling of the old cathedral

Close-up of the mosaic

Planning a Pilgrimage

Besides St. Mary's Coptic Church, pilgrims to Cairo could see some of the world's oldest paintings of the Virgin Mary at El-Ezbaweya Church and at the El-Seryan Monastery in El-Natroun Valley.

Cairo is home to one of the wonders of the world. The three pyramids of Giza were built as tombs for the pharaohs 2,600 years before the birth of Christ. The largest of these masterpieces of geometric precision is the Great Pyramid or the Pyramid of Cheops, 490 feet high. The Pyramid of Chephren, the second tallest, reaches to 460 feet, and the Pyramid of Mycerinus, the smallest, is 230 feet high.

The pyramids outside Cairo

The Sphinx, once worshipped as a sun god, guards the causeway leading to the Pyramid of Chephren. This carved-rock figure of a human-headed lion is 240 feet high.

The historic city of Alexandria lies northwest of Cairo on the Mediterranean Sea. Alexander the Great, son of King Philip II of Macedonia, conquered the Persian Empire in 332 B.C. He left Jerusalem untouched, then made his way into Egypt where he founded the city that bears his name. Alexandria was a great cultural center for centuries. Its community of poets and scholars supported the world's first great library. Alexandria later became a center of Christian learning, where scholars helped standardize the text of the New Testament.

The Sphinx

CHAPTER THIRTEEN

Our Lady of Akita

AKITA, JAPAN (1973)

Statue of Our Lady of Akita

Summary

In March 1973, Sister Agnes Katsuko Sasagawa became incurably deaf while serving as a catechist in Myoko, Japan. Soon after, she experienced supernatural phenomena and received several messages from the Virgin Mary. Our Lady asked that people turn away from sin and amend their lives. As if to reflect grief over humanity's sins, a wooden statue of Our Lady in the convent chapel wept tears 101 times from 1975 to 1981. The sobering message of Akita calls us to repentance and conversion.

The Historical Context

Christianity came to Japan on August 15, 1549, when St. Francis Xavier arrived in the port of Kagoshima. As Christianity spread it also provoked opposition. In 1614 an imperial edict banned missionary activity, and thousands of Christians died as martyrs. In 1862 Pope Pius IX canonized twenty-six martyrs of Nagasaki who had been crucified in 1597.

Missionaries began to re-enter Japan after the treaties of 1858 opened the country to foreign trade. They were astonished to discover the "Hidden Christians" in O'ura, Nagasaki. For 250 years these Japanese Christians had kept their faith alive despite persecution and lack of priests. Nagasaki still remains a center of Roman Catholicism in Japan. Today less than one percent of Japan's population is Christian, with about four hundred thousand Catholics.

Painting of St. Francis Xavier bringing Christianity to Japan

The Apparition

Agnes Katsuko Sasagawa was born on May 28, 1931. In April 1949 she became paralyzed due to a mistake in anesthesia during an appendectomy. Bedridden for ten years, in September 1958 she became friendly with a Catholic nurse, Haru Watanabe, at Myoko Hospital. Agnes received instructions in the Catholic faith and was baptized on April 17, 1960. Having recovered from her paralysis, in 1962 Agnes entered the Sisters of the Immaculate Heart of Mary at Junshin in Nagasaki. But four months later she had a relapse, and returned to the Myoko clinic. In 1964 she was cured after she drank some Lourdes water.

Sister Agnes

With her health restored, Sister Agnes began working as a catechist at the Myoko Catholic Church. In March 1973 she lost her hearing, and Dr. Katsuro Sawada of the Niigata Rosai Hospital diagnosed her deafness as incurable. In the meantime Agnes had learned about the Institute of the Handmaids of the Eucharist. Bishop Ito, its founder, invited her to enter this congregation. On May 12, 1973, Agnes transferred to this community in Akita.

Sister Agnes kept a notebook called Journey of a Soul where she recorded many of the following events. The reports of Fr. Yasuda, who spent thirteen years at the convent of Yuzawadai, supplemented her journal. Fr. Yasuda then published a major study on the events of Akita, which John Haffert translated into English (1989).

According to her diary, Agnes' first extraordinary experience occurred in 1969 at the Myoko hospital. She sensed a presence to the right of her bed, and felt someone praying the rosary with her. The stranger taught her to add after each decade of the rosary the words "O my Jesus, forgive us our sins, save us from the fires of hell, lead all souls to heaven, especially those who most need your mercy." The Virgin Mary had taught those same words to the children at Fatima; however, this prayer had not yet been translated into Japanese. At first Agnes did not know who the stranger was, but later came to understand it was her guardian angel.

After this, Sister Agnes resumed her apostolic work and life continued as usual for the next few years. The extraordinary events in Akita began on June 12, 1973. Entering the convent chapel, Sister Agnes saw a brilliant light coming from the tabernacle and she prostrated herself in adoration. Two days later as Sister Agnes and her companions prayed before the Blessed Sacrament, she saw shining rays coming from the tabernacle which was enveloped by a red flame. The next day, she had a vision of celestial light in the chapel. None of the other sisters saw these things. On June 24 Sister Agnes

Interior of the convent chapel

again saw a brilliant light shining from the Blessed Sacrament. A multitude of angels surrounded the altar in adoration before the Host.

A new development began on Thursday, June 28. As Sister Agnes prayed in the chapel, her left hand began to throb with intense pain as if something had pierced it. She looked down to see that a cross-shaped wound had formed in her palm. Blood began to flow. Agnes had received the stigmata in her left hand, a reminder of the painful wounds Christ suffered in his passion.

Statue of Our Lady in the chapel

The next morning as Agnes was praying, a person appeared close to her right, telling her, "I am the one who is with you and who watches over you." Agnes came to understand this was her guardian angel.

Sister Agnes then saw a blinding light and prostrated herself to adore the Eucharist. When she lifted her eyes, she saw a soft light enveloping the altar like a mist, as if to signify the Real Presence of Jesus in the Host. Angels appeared in the light, turning toward the Blessed Sacrament and proclaiming "Holy, Holy, Holy." Sister Agnes next heard a voice praying the following prayer Bishop Ito had composed for his community.

"Most Sacred Heart of Jesus (truly) present in the Holy Eucharist, I consecrate my body and soul to be entirely one with your heart, being sacrificed at every instant on all the altars of the world and giving praise to the Father, pleading for the coming of his kingdom. Please receive this humble offering of myself. Use me as you will for the glory of the Father and the salvation of souls.

"Most Holy Mother of God, never let me be separated from your Divine Son. Please defend and protect me as your special child. Amen."

The first message from the Virgin Mary came on July 5, 1973. Sister Agnes did not see an apparition of Mary, but heard an interior voice. The Blessed Virgin told Agnes she would be healed of her deafness.

Sister Agnes was later astonished to find a cross-shaped wound in the right hand of the Virgin's statue. Blood flowed from it on July 26. The wound on the statue is apparently a mysterious sign to authenticate the supernatural origin of Mary's message. "Do not pray only because of your sins, but in reparation for the sins of all people," the angel said on Friday, July 27. Strangely, even though the statue's hand was open and pointed down, the blood that appeared on its hand never fell to the ground.

Some suggested Sister Agnes had ectoplasmic powers to transfer her own wound and blood onto the statue. But while one analysis of the blood from the statue by the University of Akita showed it to be type B, like that of Sister Agnes, analysis of another sample in 1981 showed it to be type O. The 1981 analysis also found that the tears and perspiration coming from the statue were type AB.

The angel told Sister Agnes, "The blood shed by Mary has a profound meaning. This precious blood was shed to obtain your conversion, to ask for peace and to make reparation for ingratitude and outrages toward God.... Pray in reparation for all people." The angel said that the statue would shed blood for the last time on July 27, and Sister Agnes' suffering would also end then.

Sister Agnes received a message from what she called a "voice of incredible beauty" coming from the statue of Mary on Friday, August 3, 1973. "Many people in this world make the Lord sorrowful. I desire souls to console him.... My Son and I wish for souls who will make reparation by their suffering and their poverty...for sinners and ungrateful persons."

She went on to ask for prayer and penance to avert the suffering that sin brings into the world, and warned of chastisements. She concluded by saying, "Let each one strive, according to their abilities and their situation, to offer all they have to God."

Other supernatural events began to occur two months after this message. Sister Agnes and a companion saw a dazzling light from the statue's garment and hands on September 29, 1973—the Feast of St. Michael the Archangel, the Patron of Japan. The wound had disappeared from the hand of the statue, but perspiration began to stream from its entire body. The sisters sponged it from the statue with a cotton pad. The University of Akita later analyzed the perspiration, and confirmed it was human in origin.

The statue of Our Lady as it appears weeping

The sisters then smelled a fragrance, subtler than that of a rose, violet or lily. "The fragrance will last two weeks," an angel told Sister Agnes. As predicted, the scent of perfume stopped on October 15.

Sister Agnes received the third message from the Virgin Mary on October 13, 1973. As she prayed the rosary in the chapel, Sister Agnes heard these words from the statue:

> If people do not convert their lives, the Father will allow a terrible chastisement to fall upon all humanity. It will be a punishment worse than the deluge, such as one has never seen before. Fire will fall from the sky. Much of humanity will be destroyed. Priests will die with the faithful. Those who are spared will experience so much suffering they will envy the dead. The only weapons remaining for you will be the rosary and the sign left by my Son.
>
> Pray for the bishops and priests.... Today is the last time I will speak to you in living voice. From now on, obey your guardian

angel and your superior. Pray many rosaries. I am the only one who can save you from the misfortunes that are coming. Whoever puts their confidence in me will be saved.

Because Sister Agnes had been deaf and living in a world of silence for a year and a half, some suggest she "heard" the messages of her guardian angel and of Mary through interior locutions. That is, the voices passed through her ears, incapable of hearing, and came directly to her heart. Sister Agnes temporarily regained her hearing from October 1974 to March 1975. She was finally cured of it on Sunday, May 30, 1982, the feast of Pentecost.

The statue of Mary wept for the first time on January 4, 1975, and wept intermittently until 1981. An angel told Sister Agnes Our Lady wept to revive the faith and even if only one person converted, she cherished this.

The statue had not wept for more than a year when Sister Agnes was in the chapel on May 1, 1976. She saw tears flow once more from the statue. An angel appeared to Sister Agnes after Communion and said:

> Many people in this world cause Our Lord to suffer. Our Lady awaits souls to console him. Remain in poverty, sanctify yourself and pray in reparation for humanity's ingratitude and outrages. The rosary is your weapon. Say it carefully for the intentions of the Pope, of bishops and priests.
>
> You must never forget Mary's words. The Blessed Virgin prays continually for the conversion of the greatest possible number. She weeps, hoping to lead to Jesus and to the Father, souls offered to them by her intercession.

The statue wept for the 101st and last time on September 15, 1981—the feast of Our Lady of Sorrows. Television crews and photographers have documented the statue's tears; so have more than five hundred witnesses. The tears have flowed only from the eyes of the Virgin Mary. Medical tests at the University of Akita confirmed that the tears from the statue were human in origin but were not from Sister Agnes. The statue's tears were type AB; those of Sister Agnes were type B. Furthermore, the statue had wept even when Sister Agnes was visiting her family more than 250 miles away.

Miraculous Cures

The first miracle attributed to Our Lady of Akita was the curing of Sister Agnes' deafness. The 1981 cure of Teresa Chun, a Korean woman who suffered from a brain tumor that made her comatose, was another early miracle. Friends and family placed a picture of Our Lady of Akita under her pillow, and prayed for Teresa's recovery. She soon regained consciousness, her health restored. X rays of Teresa Chun confirmed her cure was complete.

The Recognition Process

Bishop Ito established the first commission of inquiry into the Akita apparitions in 1976. That commission declared it could not prove the events of Akita were supernatural. After seeking advice from the Vatican's Congregation for the Doctrine of the Faith, Bishop Ito established a second commission in 1979. Four of its members voted to recognize the events as supernatural; three did not.

Bishop John Ito issued a pastoral letter declaring the events of Akita to be supernatural on Easter Sunday, April 22, 1984. His letter noted the miraculous cures of both Sister Agnes and a Ko-

Entrance to the shrine

rean woman. He concluded by authorizing throughout the entire diocese the veneration of the Holy Mother of Akita and emphasized that it was a private revelation worthy of belief but was not a matter of doctrine. Bishop Ito came with a group of pilgrims to pray at the Yuzawadai sanctuary in November 1984.

Akita was the first apparition the Catholic Church has recognized in the fifty years since the apparitions at Banneux, Belgium. In 1988 Bishop Ito traveled to Rome for a meeting, and later stated that Cardinal Ratzinger had shown no disapproval of his pastoral letter.

Entrance to the garden of Akita in winter

The Shrine

The convent of the Handmaids of the Eucharist at Yuzawadai sits along a hill on the outskirts of Akita in the northwest mountain range on Kyushu island, facing the Inland Sea.

Shortly after his arrival in 1974, Fr. Yasuda initiated a project to build a beautiful Japanese garden at the convent's entrance. Inaugurated on October 11, 1975, the Garden of Mary serves as a place of repose for those who come to meditate on the events at Akita.

The statue in the Garden of Mary

Hundreds of stones have been brought from the River Kosa at the foot of Mount Chokai to landscape the grounds. Many trees have been planted in a way to preserve a view of Mount Taihei from the convent.

A pool in the form of the Japanese archipelago forms the principal part of the garden. A statue of Mary rises in the center of the garden, and a rounded hill covered in grass recalls the Sermon on the Mount. Two Japanese bridges separate the extremities of the pool from the center, symbolizing the island of Kyu-

*One of the stones brought from the River Kosa
to landscape the Garden of Mary*

shu to the south and that of Hokkaido to the north. Two cedar trunks from Akita, several hundred years old, form the entrance gate.

One can see the wooden statue of the Virgin Mary, the intermediary for the messages to Sister Agnes, in the convent chapel. The statue shows Mary standing barefoot on a globe of the world symbolizing she is the mother of all humanity. She stands before a cross as she did at Calvary.

Mr. Saburo Wakasa sculptured the statue, about twenty-seven inches high, from Katsura wood in 1965. Mary's statue looks alive at times. The garment and hair retain a color of natural wood whereas her face, hands, and feet are distinguished by a dark reddish-brown tint—much to the surprise of the sculptor when he saw the statue after a period of eight years. The wood is known for not being able to shed water.

About two and a half miles from the chapel, an abandoned farmhouse has been converted for use by the Handmaids and by the increasing number of Akita pilgrims.

Planning a Pilgrimage

Akita, with a population of three hundred thousand, is in northwestern Honshu and borders the Sea of Japan. It is easily accessible from Tokyo by plane, train or car.

Akita celebrates the Kanto festival from August 5–7. Young men balance tall bamboo poles that support lighted paper lanterns on its crossbars.

Northeast of Akita is Towado-ku Lake, Japan's third-deepest lake, offering swimming and scenic lake cruises.

Aomori, in northernmost Honshu, provides four-hour ferry service to Hakodate on the island of Hokkaido, and connections to cities such as Saporro, home of the 1972 Winter Olympics. Aomori is a center of lumbering and apple growing. The nearby Hakkoda Mountains have several hot spring resorts.

Niigata lies south of Akita on the Japan Sea, and two hours from Tokyo by express train. Niigata is the main port for ferry and hydrofoil services to Sado Island.

Cathedral of Tokyo

Cathedral of Hiroshima

Matsushima, south of Akita, in eastern Honshu, is considered one of Japan's loveliest sights. There, one can view the Pine Islands, formed into unusual formations as a result of centuries of wind and wave action.

Important Christian post-secondary institutions in Japan are found in Tokyo (such as Sophia University, a Jesuit institution of higher learning; the International Christian University; and Rikkyo University, also known as St. Paul's University) and Kyoto (Doshi-sha University).

In Nagasaki, the shrine of Our Lady of Japan was constructed in 1897 to commemorate the 17th century Japanese martyrs. It was later designated a cathedral, and fortunately most of it survived the devastation from the atomic bomb. At the Cathedral in Osaka, the pilgrim can view beautiful paintings of the Virgin Mary dressed in a kimono.

Japan has several cathedrals dedicated to Mary of the Immaculate Conception. These include the cathedrals in Tokyo, Osaka and Nagasaki. The cathedral of Hiroshima is dedicated to Our Lady of the Assumption.

Painting of Our Lady of Japan in the Cathedral of Osaka

*Nagasaki Cathedral stained glass
window over the main altar*

Atomic bomb dome in Hiroshima Peace Park

CHAPTER FOURTEEN

Our Lady, Reconciler of All People and Nations

BETANIA, VENEZUELA (1976–1984)

Grotto of Betania

Summary

The Mother of God first appeared to Maria Esperanza Medrano de Bianchini on March 25, 1976, at her farm near the parish of Cua, Venezuela. Over a hundred others saw apparitions of Mary there on March 25, 1984. Our Lady called for conversion and a return to the sacraments, especially Reconciliation and the Eucharist.

"I am Mary, Virgin and Mother of Reconciliation of all People," the Blessed Virgin told Maria Esperanza. Our Mother stressed the importance of forgiveness and love for true reconciliation.

The Historical Context

Betania is the name of a *finca* or farm located seven miles from the village of Cua in Miranda state, Venezuela, about two hours by car southwest from Caracas. It is in the diocese of Los Teques. The story of the Betania apparitions has been documented in Spanish by Pio Bello Ricardo, the bishop of Los Teques, and by Fr. Otty Ossa Aristizabal, the priest of the Betania parish. Sister Margaret Catherine Sims and Michael Brown have provided reports in English.

The name "Betania" is Spanish for Bethany, the town near Jerusalem where Jesus raised Lazarus from the dead. "I am the resurrection and the life; whoever believes in me, even if he dies, will live, and everyone who lives and believes in me will never die," Jesus told Martha, the brother of Lazarus, at Bethany (Jn 11:25).

Countryside at Betania

Entrance to the grotto

The principal visionary of the Virgin's appearances at Betania was Maria Esperanza. Born November 22, 1928, in Barrancas, the diocese of Ciudad Bolivar, Venezuela, Maria was blessed with spiritual gifts from an early age. When she was ten, her family moved to Caracas. There, she became seriously ill with bronchial pneumonia. During this illness, Maria first saw the Virgin Mary, who told her she would recover.

Maria fell seriously ill again at age fourteen, this time with heart problems. Close to death, she saw a vision of the Sacred Heart of Jesus who said he would heal her. She was instantly cured, to her doctors' amazement.

Maria decided to enter the Franciscan Sisters of Merida in Los Andes. But on October 3, 1954, Maria had a vision of St. Thérèse, who said Maria's vocation was to be a wife and mother.

Soon after this, Maria went to Rome where she met Geo Bianchini, and they married on December 8, 1956. It was the first marriage ever held in the Chapel of the Immaculate Conception in St. Peter's Basilica. While in Italy, Maria Esperanza met Padre Pio, a famous Italian mystic priest. Padre Pio suffered from the stigmata or supernatural wounds on the forehead, hands and feet. They bled profusely and corresponded to those Christ suffered during the crucifixion. The priest told Maria he had been expecting her visit, and gave her sound spiritual advice.

In Rome, Maria Esperanza dreamed in detail of a farm she would eventually buy to serve as a refuge for prayer. The Blessed Virgin described a rocky grotto in a grove of fruit trees of mangos, tangerines, avocados and bananas. Nearby a spring and a river flowed past humble dwellings. Our Lady told Maria she would appear when this property was found and be visible to many who came there to pray.

Back in Venezuela, Maria and Geo Bianchini eventually found a farm near Cua meeting the Virgin's description. They purchased it with the help of two other families in March 1974.

For most of 1975 and 1976, Maria and Geo lived in Rome, caring for her husband's bedridden mother. Maria briefly visited Caracas in February 1976, then permanently returned to Venezuela in 1977. They began to spend most weekends and holy days at Betania.

Apparition site at Betania

The Apparition

Maria saw a large cloud hovering over trees at her Betania farm at 8:30 A.M. on the feast of the Annunciation, March 25, 1976. The cloud opened and Maria saw the Virgin Mary, dressed in white, with gentle brown eyes and chestnut hair falling over her shoulders. Our Lady looked about sixteen years old. She wore a veil and had a white mantle over her shoulders. Rays of light spread in all directions from Mary's hands, similar to her 1830 appearance at Rue du Bac in Paris. The Virgin's whole being radiated light, and Maria felt as if rays of the light penetrated her soul. She trembled. The Blessed Virgin then told Maria:

> Little daughter, you are seeing me with my hands outstretched with graces and wrapped in the radiance of light to call all my children to conversion. This is the seed of glory I offer my children as Mary, Virgin and Mother, Reconciler of People, because I come to reconcile them.... Little daughter, take my message to everyone. I will protect them here in my heart from this day, forever.

Maria considered the Blessed Virgin's presence an invitation to surrender to the Lord and to accept his will.

The Virgin Mary asked Maria to erect a cross at the entrance to the apparition site in early August 1976. The Blessed Virgin then appeared to Maria on August 22. As at Lourdes, she wore a blue sash at her waist and told Maria:

> When all people take up their cross lovingly, there will be no more pain, weeping, nor death because they will live rising each day with my beloved Son in a continuous and living alleluia. I want you to help them experience the value of prayer and the importance of my recent apparition as Reconciler of People, so they will find the essential conditions to prepare their souls to receive the grace of the Holy Spirit. Prepare your souls to receive these graces by praying for faith. Little daughter, faith is the foundation of the Christian. An increase in faith will make them seek with sincere love my Father and the heart of my Divine Son joined with mine.

The Blessed Virgin again appeared to Maria on March 25, 1977, in the presence of thirty others who were praying the rosary in front of the grotto. Then, on November 27, 1977, the feastday in honor of Mary's appearance at Rue du Bac, Maria learned the Virgin would appear to her on March 25, 1978.

When the day arrived, Maria and her friends noticed a radiant mist coming toward them from the woods as they prayed at the grotto. Maria saw the Blessed Virgin, who opened her hands, emitting rays of light. Then fire seemed to consume the area, and the sun began to gyrate as people shouted. Falling to the ground,

Maria heard the Virgin tell her, "Accept the difficult task of bringing my message of love and reconciliation to the people of all nations."

Crowds at Midnight Mass

Six years later, again on the feast of the Annunciation, about 150 people participated in the Mass at Betania on March 25, 1984. Around 3:00 P.M. children praying at the spring's grotto cried out, saying they had seen the Blessed Virgin. Maria and her friends ran to the grotto where they saw Our Lady some five hundred feet away. The people described her as Our Lady of Lourdes because she wore a blue sash.

More than one hundred people witnessed Our Lady appear at the grotto seven times from 3:00 P.M. to sunset. The first six apparitions lasted ten to fifteen minutes each and the seventh, half an hour. The visionaries—including doctors, lawyers, army officers, engineers and students—submitted written testimonies to the bishop.

In the first message, the Virgin Mary told Maria Esperanza:

I am giving you a place of heaven. Lourdes…Betania of Venezuela is a place for everyone, not only Catholics. There is no distinction of classes, nations, religions…. This land is for gathering all who wish to enter. This will be a place of belief, of prayer, of faith, love and charity…. The maternal water I am handing over is the water of life. It is the water of health, of Baptism. It is the origin of your life in Christ. It will be the water of pardon that will wash away your faults and will renew you.

In the second message, the Blessed Mother told Maria Esperanza:

I have come to lead you, so that you can call my children to this place of the holy waters of my hope. It will become a place of cool relief, harmony and peace for those who come in search of this Mother, the shepherdess of souls. I have also come to ease the burdens of my priestly sons because it is they who, responding to my call, will have to make my place, chosen for these times of great disasters for humanity, the sacred enclosure where all my children will find refuge to rebuild the walls of the triumphant New Jerusalem. All have to be saved by the faith, love and truth of a people appealing for justice.

In Mary's third message to Maria Esperanza at Betania, she said:

Children, you will never be perfect because as long as there is flesh and blood, you all have to pass through stages and years of learning. You must hunger for God. Children, as Mary, Mother and Reconciler of Nations, I come to reconcile them, to seek them out, to give them faith—the faith that has disappeared in the noise of an atomic awakening at the point of exploding. There must be forgiveness, reflecting that only love can save humanity.

Those who, repentant and weeping over their evil ways, turn their eyes to the grotto of my apparition, asking me for forgiveness, will receive an abundance of graces. Their souls will remain pure and clean like the day they were cleansed in holy Baptism. All will be resurrected with my Son and with him, you are going to obtain the model of perfect Christianity—Christ my divine Son in you.

In the fourth message, Mary asked for help in building her house in this place. She called it:

…a refuge of a Mother with the title, Mary, Reconciler of People and Nations. Pray, meditate and nourish yourselves with the bread of the Eucharist that gives supernatural life. People need to find themselves, seeing each person as one's own brother or sister…to recognize each one as a member of the same family, the family of

God. I am your Mother who comes to seek you so that you may prepare yourselves and bring my message of reconciliation. The conscience of the people must be violently shaken so they can put their life in order and offer to Jesus the just reparation for the daily infidelities committed by sinners.

Mary asked for reconciliation among people and nations in the fifth message, warning that if people do not convert, their sins will cause suffering.

Miraculous Cures

The Ecks (1993) report several miracles; some of those occurred immediately after an ill person drank water from the spring at Betania. For example, a woman who could not speak and was paralyzed from her waist down recovered within a day of drinking water a friend had brought from Betania.

A surgeon from a hospital in Maracaibo, Venezuela, had prostate cancer and only a few years to live. At Betania, he had a vision of Mary radiating a beautiful light. He felt an infusion of heat in his body, and tests later showed he was cured.

Cases of advanced cancer of the kidneys and of duodenal ulcers have also been reported miraculously cured.

Mountain spring to the right of the grotto

Fountains at Betania

The Recognition Process

Bishop Pio Bello Ricardo, the bishop of Los Teques diocese, investigated the apparitions himself, without a commission. He interviewed more than two hundred witnesses and analyzed 380 written declarations, some of them from groups. The bishop estimated that five hundred people had seen the Betania apparition by 1987. No evidence of mystical or ecstatic trances could be found among the visionaries, he pointed out, but many noted the fragrance of roses and the singing of invisible choirs. Bishop Pio was certain the events were supernatural, not a case of fraud, collective suggestion, or promotion of group interests.

Bishop Pio declared the Betania apparitions worthy of belief in a pastoral letter dated November 21, 1987—a particularly fitting time, as it fell during the Marian Year declared by Pope John Paul II. Bishop Pio wrote: "I therefore approve, officially, that the site of the apparitions be considered sacred and kept as a place for pilgrimages, a place of prayer, reflection and worship where liturgical acts may be performed, especially the celebration of the Mass and the administration of the sacraments of Reconciliation and the Eucharist." The bishop did not simply confirm that the apparitions were worthy of belief, should people so choose. He attested to their authenticity, something that the Church had not done for any apparitions since those in Belgium in the 1930s.

Thanksgiving plaques for favors received

The Shrine

Facilities at Betania are simple and sparse. A large outdoor altar with a tin roof can shelter four hundred people from the rain. Nearby, a grotto carved from the rocks holds a statue of Our Lady of Lourdes. Hundreds of votive candles and flowers surround the grotto, while a mountain spring cascades water to its right.

There are no restaurants but a few food stands can be found near the entrance to the sanctuary. The grounds have rest rooms but no sleeping accommodations. International pilgrims usually stay in Caracas and make the two-hour trip to Betania by car or bus.

In 1989, the bishop announced plans to build a permanent chapel at Betania in honor of Mary's appearance there. The cornerstone was laid in 1992 for the Church of Mary, Virgin and Mother of Reconciliation of All People.

The new chapel at Betania

Main altar inside the chapel

*Festive banner hanging
in the chapel*

About twenty thousand pilgrims attended a Mass concelebrated by seven bishops and priests from many countries on March 25, 1994, the feast of the Annunciation.

Planning a Pilgrimage

Most foreign pilgrims will arrive at the Simon Bolivar International Airport, a half-hour cab ride from Caracas, Venezuela's capital city of four million.

The pilgrim could visit the Cathedral of Caracas, near the Plaza Bolivar, the city's historical center. Completed in 1595, the cathedral was partially destroyed by an earthquake, then rebuilt.

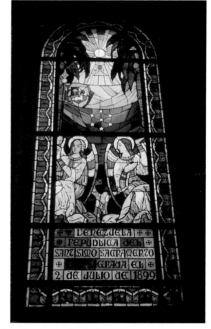

Stained glass windows in the Cathedral of Caracas

*Famous carved wood altar in
San Francisco Church (Caracas)*

Nearby is the famous San Francisco Church with its stunning wooden altar, built in the 16th century.

Among many museums in Caracas are the *Museo del Arte Colonial,* the *Museo de Bellas Artes,* the *Museo de Ciencias Naturales,* the *Galeria de Arte Nacional,* and the *Museo de Arte Contemporaneo.* The University of Caracas is worth seeing for its contemporary architecture, murals, sculptures and frescoes.

The shrine of Our Lady of Coromoto is found in Guanara, Venezuela, and is based on an apparition of Our Blessed Mother to the chief of the Guanara tribe on September 8, 1652. Today a statue of the Virgin with the Christ Child is venerated at the shrine.

Close to Los Teques is the town of Tumero. There, a copy of a picture of *Nuestra Senora del Perpetuo Socorro* (Our Lady of Perpetual Help) found in Damascus has been emitting oil for several years. Many miraculous cures have been attributed to the healing power of this oil.

If time permits, the tourist can make a side trip to Margarita Island, discovered by Columbus in 1498. *Margarita* is the Greek word for "pearl," and pearls played an important role early in the island's history. Only forty-three miles long, the island has eighteen official beaches. The flight from Caracas is less than an hour and the ride to its main city of Porlamar is another half-hour. Nearby, in the town of El Valle, is the Church of Our Lady of the Valley with many beautiful paintings.

Asuncion Church on Margarita Island

Six miles northeast of Porlamar is Pampatar, with its fort of San Carlos Borromeo. The colonial town also has an old church with the statue of "Christ of the Happy Voyage," originally destined for Peru, but unloaded in Margarita because of a storm. Also north of Porlamar is the colonial town of La Asuncion with one of Venezuela's oldest churches, the *Nuestra Senora de la Asuncion* dating from 1599.

Sunset over Margarita Island

APPENDIX

THE SHRINE

Memory, Presence and Prophecy
of the Living God

PONTIFICAL COUNCIL FOR THE
PASTORAL CARE OF
MIGRANTS AND ITINERANT PEOPLE

Contents

Introduction

1. The Meaning and Aim of the Document

"All Christians are invited to become part of the great pilgrimage that Christ, the Church and mankind have made and must continue to make in history. The shrine which is the goal of that pilgrimage is to become 'the Tent of Meeting,' as the Bible calls the tabernacle of the covenant."[1] These words invite us to consider the relationship between the notion of pilgrimage[2] and that of the shrine, which is usually the visible goal of the pilgrim's journey: "The term 'shrine' designates a church or other sacred place to which the faithful make pilgrimages for a particular religious reason, with the approval of the local Ordinary."[3] In shrines, a meeting with the living God can take place through the life-giving experience of the *Mystery* which is proclaimed, celebrated and lived: "At shrines, the means of salvation are to be provided more abundantly to the faithful; the Word of God is to be carefully proclaimed; liturgical life is to be appropriately fostered, especially through the celebration of the Eucharist and penance; and approved forms of popular devotion are to be cultivated."[4] "Shrines are thus like milestones that

---

1. Pontifical Council for the Pastoral Care of Migrants and Itinerant People, *Pilgrimage in the Great Jubilee of the Year 2000* (April 11, 1998), 32; the text refers to Ex 27:21; 29:4, 10–11, 30, 32, 42, 44.

2. Cf. *ibid.*; Document of the Italian Episcopal Conference, *"Venite, saliamo sul monte del Signore" (Is 2, 3). Il pellegrinaggio alle soglie del terzo millennio* (June 29, 1998).

3. *Code of Canon Law,* can. 1230.

4. *Ibid.*, can. 1234, §1.

guide the journey of the children of God on earth";[5] they foster the experience of gathering and encounter, and the building up of the ecclesial community.

These characteristics apply in a unique way to the shrines that have sprung up in the Holy Land, in the places sanctified by the presence of the Word Incarnate, and they can be seen particularly in the places consecrated by the martyrdom of the apostles and all those who bore witness to the faith by shedding their blood. One can also find the entire history of the pilgrim Church reflected in countless shrines, "permanent witnesses of the Good News,"[6] linked to the decisive events of the evangelization or the faith life of different peoples and communities. Every shrine can be seen as the bearer of a specific message, since it vividly makes present today the foundational event of the past which still speaks to the heart of pilgrims. Marian shrines in particular provide an authentic school of faith based on Mary's example and motherly intercession. Today too, by their witness to the manifold richness of God's saving activity, all shrines are an inestimable gift of grace to his Church.

A reflection on the nature and purpose of shrines can thus be an effective aid in receiving and living out the great gift of reconciliation and new life that the Church continually offers to all the disciples of the Redeemer and, through them, to the whole human family. This then is the underlying *meaning and aim* of the present document; it wishes to consider the flowering of the spiritual life that takes place at shrines, the pastoral activity of those who minister in them, and their effects on the life of the local Churches.

The following reflection is only a modest aid toward a greater appreciation of the service that shrines render to the life of the Church.

2. Listening to God's Revelation

If reflection on shrines is to nourish faith and prove fruitful for pastoral activity, it needs to be rooted in an *obedient listening to revelation*, which richly presents the message and the power of salvation contained in the "mystery of the Temple."

---

5. Pope John Paul II, *Homily* in Corrientes, Argentina (April 9, 1987).
6. Pope John Paul II, *Angelus* (July 12, 1992).

In the language of the Bible, and especially of St. Paul, the term "mystery" refers to God's plan of salvation unfolding in human history. When we contemplate the "mystery of the Temple" in attentive listening to the Word of God, we can glimpse, beyond the visible events of history, the presence of the divine "glory" (cf. Ps 29:9): the manifestation of the God who is thrice holy (cf. Is 6:3), his presence in dialogue with mankind (cf. 1 Kg 8:30–53), his entry into time and space, his planting his "tent" in our midst (cf. Jn 1:14). The outline of a theology of the temple thus emerges, in the light of which we can better understand the significance of the shrine.

This theology is characterized by a growing concentration upon certain focal points: in the first place, the figure of the "cosmic temple," evoked for example by Psalm 19 with its image of the "two suns," the sun of the Torah—or of the revelation explicitly addressed to Israel (vv. 7–14)—and the sun in the heavens which "declare the glory of God" (vv. 1–6) in a revelation that is silent yet universal, effective and directed to all. Within this temple the divine presence is everywhere felt (cf. Ps 139) and a liturgy of ecstatic praise is celebrated, as Psalm 148 makes clear, since together with the creatures of heaven, it mentions a universal *"alleluia"* intoned by twenty-two earthly creatures—as many as the letters of the Hebrew alphabet—thus signifying the whole of creation.

Then there is the temple of Jerusalem, where the Ark of the Covenant was kept, the holy place *par excellence* of the Jewish faith and the permanent memorial of the God of history, who established a covenant with his people and remains ever faithful to it. The temple is the visible house of the Eternal One (Ps 11:4), filled by the cloud of his presence (cf. 1 Kg 8:10–13) and the dwelling place of his "glory" (cf. 1 Kg 8:11).

Finally, there is the new and definitive temple which is the eternal Son, who came in the flesh (cf. Jn 1:14), the Lord Jesus, crucified and risen (cf. Jn 2:19–21), who makes of those who believe in him a temple built of living stones, which is the pilgrim Church in time: "He is the living stone, rejected by human beings but chosen by God and precious to him; come to him so that you, too, may be living stones making a spiritual house as a holy priesthood to offer the spiritual sacrifices made acceptable to God through Jesus Christ" (1 Pet 2:4–5). By drawing close to the One who is the "living stone," we construct the spiritual building of the new and perfect covenant.

We also prepare for the feast of the Kingdom that is "not yet" fully realized, thanks to our spiritual sacrifices (cf. Rom 12:1–2), which are pleasing to God precisely because they are offered in Christ, through him and with him, the Covenant in person. The Church thus appears above all as "the holy temple, visibly represented in the shrines of stone."[7]

3. The Supporting Arches

In the light of these scriptural testimonies, we can come to a deeper understanding of the "mystery of the Temple" in three ways, which correspond to the three dimensions of time and which serve as the *supporting arches* of a theology of the shrine, namely, *memory, presence and prophecy* of the God who is with us.

In relation to the unique and definitive *past* of the event of our salvation, the shrine appears as a *memory* of our origin with the Lord of heaven and earth. In relation to the *present* of the community of the redeemed, gathered in the time between the first and the final coming of the Lord, the shrine appears as a sign of the divine *Presence,* the place of the covenant, where the community of the covenant constantly expresses and renews itself. In relation to the *future* fulfillment of the promise of God, that "not yet" which is the object of our greatest hope, the shrine is set as a *prophecy* of God's tomorrow in the today of the present world.

Each of these three dimensions can inspire the outlines of a pastoral plan for shrines, one capable of translating into personal and ecclesial life the symbolic meaning of the temple, where the Christian community assembles, called together by the bishop and the priests who are his co-workers.

---

7. SECOND VATICAN ECUMENICAL COUNCIL, Dogmatic Constitution *Lumen Gentium,* 6.

I. The Shrine, a Memory of Origins

4. Memory of God's Work

A shrine is first of all a *place of memory,* the memory of God's powerful activity in history, which is the origin of the People of the Covenant and the faith of each believer.

The Patriarchs had already commemorated their encounters with God by building an altar or a memorial (cf. Gn 12:6–8; 13:18; 33:18–20), to which they would return as a sign of fidelity (cf. Gn 13:4; 46:1), and Jacob considered the place where his vision took place as a "dwelling-place of God" (cf. Gn 28:11–22). In the Biblical tradition, the shrine is not merely the work of human hands, filled with cosmological or anthropological symbolism, but a witness to God's initiative in revealing himself to human persons and making his covenant of salvation with them. The deepest meaning of every shrine is to serve as a reminder in faith of the salvific work of the Lord.[8]

In a spiritual climate of adoration, invocation and praise, Israel knew that it was her God who freely desired the Temple, not human presumption. An exemplary witness to this is the splendid prayer of Solomon, born precisely of his powerful awareness of the reality of the temptation of idolatry: "Yet will God really live with human beings on earth? Why, the heavens, the highest of the heavens cannot contain you. How much less this temple built by me! Even so, listen favorably to the prayer and entreaty of your

---

8. The various shrines of ancient Israel (Shechem, Bethel, Beersheba, Shiloh) are all linked to the stories of the Patriarchs and are memorials of the encounter with the living God.

servant, Lord, my God; listen to the cry and to the prayer which your servant makes to you today: day and night may your eyes watch over this temple, over this place of which you have said, 'My name will be there.' Listen to the prayer which your servant offers in this place" (1 Kg 8:27–29).

The shrine, then, was not built because Israel wanted to capture the presence of the Eternal, but just the opposite, because the living God, who entered history, who journeyed with his people in the cloud by day and in the fire by night (cf. Ex 13:21), wanted to give a sign of his fidelity and his continual active presence in the midst of his people. Thus the Temple would not be a house built by human hands, but a place that would proclaim the initiative of the One who alone builds the house. This is the simple yet grand truth expressed in the words spoken to the prophet Nathan: "Go and tell my servant David, 'The Lord says this: Are you to build a temple for me to live in?... The Lord furthermore tells you that he will make of you a dynasty. And when your days are over and you fall asleep with your ancestors, I shall appoint your heir, your own son to succeed you, and I shall make his sovereignty secure. He will build a temple for my name and I shall make his royal throne secure forever. I shall be a father to him and he a son to me'" (2 Sam 7:5, 11–14).

The shrine thus becomes a sort of living *memorial* of the origin from on high of the chosen and beloved People of the Covenant. It is a permanent reminder of the fact that God's people is born not of flesh or blood (cf. Jn 1:13), but that the life of faith is born of the wondrous initiative of God, who entered history to unite us to himself and to change our hearts and our lives. The shrine is the efficacious *memorial* of God's work, the visible sign proclaiming to all generations how great is his love and testifying that he first loved us (cf. 1 Jn 4:19) and wishes to be the Lord and Savior of his people. As Gregory of Nyssa said in reference to the shrines of the Holy Land, in every shrine one can recognize "traces of the great goodness of the Lord for us," "the salvific signs of God who gave us life,"[9] "the memories of the mercy of the Lord in our regard."[10]

---

9. *Epist.* 3, 1: *Sources Chrétiennes,* 363, 124.

10. *Ibid.,* 3, 2: *SCh* 363, 126.

5. An Initiative "from Above"

What the Temple of Jerusalem signified in the Old Testament finds its highest fulfillment in the New Testament, in the mission of the Son of God. He himself becomes the new Temple, the dwelling of the Eternal One among us, the Covenant in person. The episode of the expulsion of the vendors from the temple (cf. Mt 21:12–13) declares that the sacred space, on the one hand, has been extended to all peoples, as we see from a detail of great symbolical value, namely, that the veil of the temple was "torn in two from top to bottom" (Mk 15:38). On the other hand, the sacred space is concentrated in the person of the One who—victorious over death (cf. 2 Tim 1:10)—comes to be the sacrament of the encounter with God for everyone.

To the religious leaders, Jesus said: "Destroy this Temple, and in three days I will raise it up." Citing their reply—"It has taken forty-six years to build this Temple: are you going to raise it up again in three days?"—John the Evangelist comments: "But he was speaking of the Temple that was his body, and when Jesus rose from the dead, his disciples remembered that he had said this, and they believed the Scripture and what he had said" (Jn 2:19–22).

In the economy of the new Covenant too, the Temple is the sign of the initiative of God's love in history: Christ, the one sent by the Father, God made man for us, the eternal high priest (cf. Heb 7), is the new Temple, the awaited and promised Temple, the sanctuary of the new and eternal covenant (cf. Heb 8). Both in the Old and in the New Testament, therefore, the shrine is a living *memorial* of the origin, of the initiative by which God loved us first (1 Jn 4:19).Whenever Israel looked at the Temple with the eyes of faith, whenever Christians look in the same way at Christ, the new Temple, and at the shrines that, from the edict of Constantine on, they have built as a sign of the living Christ among us, they recognize in this sign the initiative of the love of the living God for mankind.[11]

The shrine thus testifies that God is greater than our heart, that he has always loved us and has given us his Son and the Holy

---

11. In shrines, it is possible "to enkindle the fire of divine love in every home," as Theodoret of Cyr observes with regard to the Church built in honor of St. Thecla (*Historia Religiosa, 29, 7: SCh 257, 239*).

Spirit because he wants to dwell in us, making us his temple and making our bodies the shrine of the Holy Spirit. As St. Paul says: "Do you not realize that you are a temple of God with the Spirit of God living in you? If anybody should destroy the temple of God, God will destroy that person, because God's temple is holy; and you are that temple" (1 Cor 3:16–17; cf. 6:19). "The temple of God...is what we are—the temple of the living God, as he himself has said: *I shall fix my home among them and live among them; I will be their God and they will be my people*" (2 Cor 6:16).

The shrine is the place where the love of God, who has planted his tent among us (cf. Jn 1:14), is constantly made present. Therefore, as St. Augustine says, in the holy place "there is no succession of days as if each day were to come and then go. The beginning of one does not mark the end of the other, because there all of them will be present at one and the same time. The life to which those days belong will know no setting."[12] Thus, in ever new ways, the shrine resounds with the joyful proclamation that "God loved us first and gave us the capacity to love him.... He did not love us in order to leave us as ugly as we were, but to transform us and make us beautiful.... How shall we be beautiful? By loving him, who is ever beautiful. In the measure that love grows in you, in the same measure will your beauty grow; for charity is truly the beauty of the soul."[13] A shrine thus constantly reminds us that new life is not born "from below" by purely human initiative, and that the Church is not simply a product of flesh and blood (cf. Jn 1:13), but rather that the life of the redeemed and the ecclesial communion in which that life finds expression are born "from above" (cf. Jn 3:3), from the gratuitous and amazing initiative of trinitarian love that is prior to all human love (cf. 1 Jn 4:9–10).

6. Awe and Adoration

What are the consequences for our Christian life of this first and fundamental message that the shrine transmits, insofar as it is a *memory* of our origin in the Lord?

We can speak of three fundamental approaches.

---

12. St. Augustine, *Letter to Proba*, 130, 8, 15.
13. St. Augustine, *Commentary on the Letter of John*, IX, 9.

In the first place, the shrine reminds us that the Church is born of God's initiative, an initiative that the piety of the faithful and the public approval of the Church acknowledge in the foundational event at the origin of every shrine. Thus, in everything associated with the shrine and in everything that finds expression in it, we need to discern the presence of the mystery, the activity of God in time, the manifestation of his efficacious presence, hidden under the signs of history. This conviction is further expressed in the shrine through the specific message connected with it, whether in regard to the mysteries of the life of Jesus Christ, in regard to one of the titles of Mary, "who shines forth to the whole community of the elect as a model of the virtues,"[14] or in regard to the individual saints whose memory proclaims the "wonderful works of Christ in his servants."[15]

One approaches the mystery with an attitude of *awe* and *adoration,* with a sense of *wonder* before the gift of God; for this reason, one enters a shrine with a spirit of adoration. Anyone who is incapable of experiencing wonder at the work of God, who does not perceive the newness of what God brings about through his loving initiative, will not be capable of perceiving the profound significance and beauty of the mystery of the Temple, which is disclosed in the shrine. The proper respect shown to a holy place expresses the awareness that, in seeing what God has done, we need to respond not with a human logic, which presumes to define everything on the basis of what is seen and produced, but with an attitude of veneration, filled with awe and a sense of mystery.

Surely, an adequate *preparation* is needed for an encounter with a shrine, so that we can perceive beyond its visible, artistic and folkloric aspects the gracious work of God evoked by various signs, such as apparitions, miracles, the foundational events that represent the real first beginnings of every shrine as a place of faith.

This preparation will take place, first of all, during the stops in the journey that leads the pilgrim to the shrine; such was the case for the pilgrims to Zion who prepared themselves for the great meeting

---

14. SECOND VATICAN ECUMENICAL COUNCIL, Dogmatic Constitution *Lumen Gentium,* 65.

15. SECOND VATICAN ECUMENICAL COUNCIL, Constitution *Sacrosanctum Concilium,* 111.

with the Shrine of God by singing the Psalms of Ascent (Pss 120–134), which are a true liturgical catechesis on the conditions, nature and effects of an encounter with the mystery of the Temple.

The topographical arrangement of the shrine and its individual areas, the respectful behavior that is required of every ordinary visitor, the attentive hearing of the Word of God, prayer and the celebration of the sacraments will prove of immense help in enabling people to understand the spiritual significance of their experience there. All these actions together can express the spirit of welcome radiated by the shrine, which is open to everyone and, in particular, to the many people who in the loneliness of a secularized and desacralized world perceive deep in their hearts a yearning for and an attraction to holiness.[16]

7. Thanksgiving

In the second place, a shrine recalls God's initiative and makes us understand that that initiative, the fruit of a pure gift, must be received in the spirit of *thanksgiving*.

One enters a shrine above all to give thanks, conscious that God loved us even before we were capable of loving him; to express our praise of the Lord for his marvelous works (cf. Ps 136); to ask his forgiveness for the sins we have committed; and to implore the gift of fidelity in our life as believers and the help needed as we make our earthly pilgrimage.

In this sense, shrines represent an extraordinary school of prayer, where the persevering and trusting attitude of the humble testifies in a special way to their faith in the Lord's promise: "Ask and it shall be given to you" (Mt 7:7).[17]

To recognize the shrine as a *memory* of God's initiative is thus to learn the art of thanksgiving, to foster in our hearts a spirit of reconciliation, contemplation and peace. A shrine reminds us that joy in life is first of all the effect of the presence of the Holy Spirit

---

16. Cf. Pope John Paul II, *Homily* at the Shrine of Belém, Brazil (July 8, 1980).

17. The *Catechism of the Catholic Church* notes that "for pilgrims who are in search of their own living springs, shrines are exceptional places where the various forms of Christian prayer may be lived 'as Church'" (2691).

who also awakens in us the praise of God. The more we are enabled to praise the Lord and make our life a continuous act of thanksgiving to the Father (cf. Rom 12:1) in union with the one and perfect thanksgiving of Christ the priest, in particular through the celebration of the Eucharist, the more will we welcome God's gift within us and allow it to bear fruit.

From this standpoint, the Virgin Mary is "a most excellent model."[18] In the spirit of thanksgiving, she let herself be overshadowed by the Spirit (cf. Lk 1:35), so that in her the Word of God might be conceived and given to mankind. In gazing upon her, we understand that a shrine is a place where the gift from on high is welcomed, the dwelling in which, even as we give thanks, we allow ourselves to be loved by the Lord, following his example and with his help.

Shrines thus remind us that where there is no gratitude, the gift is lost; where man does not give thanks to the God who each day, even in the hour of trial, loves him ever anew, the gift remains ineffective.

Shrines testify that the vocation of life is not dissipation, frivolity or escape, but praise, peace and joy. A profound understanding of the meaning of a shrine can help us to experience the contemplative dimensions of life, not only inside the shrine itself but everywhere. And since the Sunday Eucharistic celebration is the culmination and source of the whole Christian life, lived as a response of gratitude and self-oblation to the gift from on high, a shrine invites us in a most particular way to rediscover Sunday, "the day of the Lord" and "lord of the days,"[19] the "primordial feast," "which is meant not only to mark the passage of time, but to reveal its profound meaning," namely, the glory of God who is all in all.[20]

---

18. SECOND VATICAN ECUMENICAL COUNCIL, Dogmatic Constitution *Lumen Gentium,* 54 and 65.

19. PSEUDO-EUSEBIUS OF ALEXANDRIA, *Sermons* 16: *PG* 86, 416.

20. Pope John Paul II writes in his Apostolic Letter *Dies Domini* (May 31, 1998), "There is also a rediscovery of ancient religious practices, such as pilgrimages; and often the faithful take advantage of Sunday rest to visit a shrine where, with the whole family perhaps, they can spend time in a more intense experience of faith. These are moments of grace which must be fostered through evangelization and guided by genuine pastoral wisdom" (52).

8. Sharing and Commitment

In the third place, as a *memory* of our origin, the shrine shows that this sense of awe and thanksgiving should never be separated from *sharing* with others and a *commitment* to others. The shrine calls to mind the gift of a God who has loved us so much that he pitched his tent among us to bring us salvation, to be our companion in life, one with us in our suffering and in our joy. The founding events of the various shrines also bear witness to this divine solidarity. If God so loved us, so too must we love others (cf. 1 Jn 4:12), so that we may be the temple of God by our lives. A shrine is an impetus to solidarity, impelling us to be "living stones" that support one another in the edifice built on the cornerstone which is Christ (1 Pet 2:4–5).

It would be fruitless to experience the "time of the shrine" if this does not then draw us to the "time of the road," the "time of the mission," and the "time of service," wherever God manifests himself as love for the weakest and poorest creatures.

The words of Jeremiah, echoed in the teaching of Jesus, remind us that a temple, without faith and without a commitment to justice, is reduced to a "den of thieves" (cf. Jer 7:11; Mt 21:13). The shrines mentioned by Amos are meaningless unless the Lord is truly sought in them. Liturgy without a life rooted in justice becomes a farce (cf. Is 1:10–20; Am 5:21–25; Hos 6:6). The words of the prophets call the shrine back to its original inspiration, stripping it of empty "sacralism" and idolatry, and making it a seed which bears the fruit of faith and justice in time and space. Then indeed the shrine, as the *memory* of our origin in the Lord, becomes a continuous call to the love of God and to the sharing of gifts received. A visit to the shrine will show its effects above all in a commitment to charitable activities, in work for the advancement of human dignity, justice and peace, values to which the faithful will feel themselves called anew.

II. The Shrine, a Place of God's Presence

9. A Place of the Covenant

The mystery of the shrine does not only call to mind our origin in the Lord; it also reminds us that once God has loved us, he never ceases to love us. In the specific moment of history in which we find ourselves today, faced with all the contradictions and the sufferings of the present, he is with us. The Old and the New Testaments bear unanimous witness that the Temple is not only a place where the saving past is remembered, but also one where grace is even now experienced. A shrine is a *sign of God's Presence,* a place where men's covenant with the Eternal One and with one another is constantly renewed. In journeying to the shrine, the pious Israelite discovered anew God's covenant fidelity to each "today" of history.[21]

As they gaze upon the Lord, the new temple whose living presence in the Spirit is evoked by every church building, Christ's followers know that God is always living and present among them and for them. The temple is the holy dwelling of the *Ark of the Covenant,* the place where the covenant with the living God is constantly renewed and the people of God become aware that they are a community of believers, "a chosen race, a kingdom of priests, a holy nation" (1 Pet 2:9). As St. Paul reminds us: "You are no longer aliens or foreign visitors; you are fellow citizens with the holy people

---

21. One thinks again of the Songs of Ascent to the temple of Jerusalem and of the image of God, the guardian of Israel, that they present (cf. esp. Pss 121 and 127).

of God and part of God's household. You are built upon the foundations of the apostles and prophets, and Christ Jesus himself is the cornerstone. Every structure knit together in him grows into a holy temple in the Lord; and you, too, in him, are being built up into a dwelling place of God in the Spirit" (Eph 2:19–22). By dwelling among his people and in their hearts, God himself makes them a living shrine. A shrine built of "dead stones" evokes the One who makes us a shrine of "living stones."[22]

A shrine is a place of the Spirit because it is a place where God's fidelity reaches out and transforms us. People go to a shrine first of all to call upon and to receive the Holy Spirit, in order then to bring this Spirit to all the activities of their lives. In this sense, a shrine appears as a constant reminder of the living presence of the Holy Spirit in the Church, bestowed upon us by the risen Christ (cf. Jn 20:22) to the glory of the Father. A shrine is a visible invitation to drink from the invisible spring of living water (cf. Jn 4:14); an invitation which can always be experienced anew, in order to live in fidelity to the covenant with the Eternal One in the Church.

10. A Place of the Word

The expression "communion of saints," found in the section of the Creed which describes the work of the Holy Spirit, can be seen as a rich evocation of one aspect of the mystery of the Church on her pilgrimage through history. By filling the members of Christ's Body, the Holy Spirit makes the Church the living temple of the Lord, as the Second Vatican Council recalled: "The Church has often been called the building of God (cf. 1 Cor 3:9).... This building has many names: the house of God (cf. 1 Tim 3:15) in which his family dwells; the household of God in the Spirit (cf. Eph 2:19–22); 'the dwelling place of God among men' (Rev 21:3); and, especially the holy temple. This temple, symbolized by places of worship built of stone, is praised by the holy Fathers and, not without reason, is compared in the liturgy to the Holy City, the New Jerusalem. As living

---

22. Gregory of Nyssa writes: "Wherever you are, God will come to you, if the dwelling in your soul is found to be such that the Lord can dwell in you" (*Epistula* 2, 16: *SCh* 363, 121).

stones we here on earth are being built up along with this City (cf. 1 Pet 2:5)."[23]

In this holy temple of the Church, the Spirit acts especially through the signs of the new covenant that shrines possess and make available. One of these is the Word of God. The shrine is the *place of the Word par excellence,* in which the Spirit calls us to faith and brings about the "communion of the faithful." It is extremely important that a shrine be associated with the persistent and receptive hearing of the Word of God, which is no mere human word, but the living God himself present in his Word. The shrine, in which the Word of God resounds, is a place of covenant, where God reminds his people of his faithfulness, in order to shed light on their journey and to offer them consolation and strength.

A shrine can become an excellent place for deepening one's faith, in a special setting and at a favorable time, apart from the ordinary. It can offer possibilities for a new evangelization, help to foster a popular piety that is "rich in values,"[24] bringing it to a more exact and mature consciousness of faith,[25] and it can facilitate the process of inculturation.[26]

Each shrine needs to develop "a suitable catechesis"[27] which, "while it is to take into account the events that are celebrated in the places to be visited and their peculiar nature, should not overlook either the necessary hierarchy in expounding the truths of the faith or its proper place within the liturgical itinerary in which the whole Church participates."[28]

---

23. SECOND VATICAN ECUMENICAL COUNCIL, Dogmatic Constitution *Lumen Gentium,* 6.

24. POPE PAUL VI, Apostolic Exhortation *Evangelii Nuntiandi* (December 8, 1975), 48.

25. Cf. POPE JOHN PAUL II, *Homily* at the Shrine of Zapopán, Mexico (January 30, 1979).

26. Cf. INTERNATIONAL THEOLOGICAL COMMISSION, Doc. *Fides et Inculturatio* (1987), III, 2–7.

27. PONTIFICAL COUNCIL FOR THE PASTORAL CARE OF MIGRANTS AND ITINERANT PEOPLE, *Walk toward the Splendor of God. Your God Walks with You.* Proceedings of the First World Congress on the Pastoral Care of Shrines and Pilgrimages (Rome, February 26–29, 1992), Final Document, 8, p. 216.

28. *Pilgrimage in the Great Jubilee of the Year 2000,* 34.

In this pastoral service of evangelization and catechesis, emphasis should be placed on the specific aspects linked to the memory of each particular shrine, to *its own* particular message, to the "charism" entrusted to it by the Lord and recognized by the Church, and to the heritage of traditions and customs, frequently very rich, that have taken root there.

In the same context of service to evangelization, cultural and artistic initiatives can be sponsored, such as congresses, seminars, exhibitions, reviews, competitions and gatherings on religious themes. "In the past, our shrines were filled with religious mosaics, paintings and sculptures, to teach the faith. Shall we have enough spiritual strength and genius to create 'moving images,' of great quality, and adapted to the culture of today? It is a question not only of the first proclamation of the faith in a world that is often very secularized, or of catechesis to deepen this faith, but it is a question of the inculturation of the Gospel message at the level of each people, of each cultural tradition."[29]

To this end, a shrine needs the presence of pastoral workers capable of helping people to enter into dialogue with God and to contemplate the immense mystery that enfolds and attracts us. The significance of the ministry of the priests, religious and communities in charge of shrines must be stressed,[30] and consequently the urgent need for them to receive proper training for the service they are called to provide. At the same time, encouragement should be given to lay people trained to carry out the work of catechesis and evangelization associated with the life of the shrine. In this way shrines too will express the wealth of charisms and ministries that the Holy Spirit awakens in the Lord's Church, and pilgrims will benefit from the varied witness given by the different pastoral workers.

---

29. Pope John Paul II, *Message for the Fiftieth Anniversary of the International Catholic Organization for Cinema* (October 31, 1978).

30. Cf. Second Vatican Ecumenical Council, Decree *Presbyterorum Ordinis,* 4.

11. A Place of Sacramental Encounter

Shrines, as places in which the Spirit speaks also through the specific message which the Church recognizes as associated with each shrine, are also *privileged places for the celebration of the sacraments*. This is especially true for the sacraments of Reconciliation and the Eucharist, in which the Word is most powerfully present and at work. The sacraments bring about an encounter of the living with the One who constantly preserves them in life and grants them ever new life in the consoling power of the Holy Spirit. They are not rote rituals, but events of salvation, personal encounters with the living God who in the Spirit goes forth to meet all those who come to him hungering and thirsting for his truth and peace. When a sacrament is celebrated in the shrine, therefore, it is not that *something* "is done," but rather that *someone* is encountered. Indeed, that someone is Christ, who becomes present in the grace of the Spirit in order to give himself to us and to change our life, incorporating us ever more fruitfully into the community of the covenant, the Church.

As a place of encounter with the Lord of life, the shrine as such is a clear sign of the presence of God at work in the midst of his people, for there, through his Word and the sacraments, he gives himself to us. Pilgrims thus approach a shrine as the Temple of the living God, the place of the living covenant with him, so that the grace of the sacraments may liberate them from sin and grant them the strength to begin again with a new freshness and new joy in their hearts, and thus to become, in the midst of the world, transparent witnesses of the Eternal.

Pilgrims often come to shrines particularly well-disposed to seek the grace of forgiveness; they should be helped to open themselves to the Father "rich in mercy" (Eph 2:4),[31] in truth and in freedom, consciously and responsibly, so that their encounter with his grace will give rise to a truly new life. A fitting community penance service could lead to a richer experience of the individual celebration of the sacrament of Reconciliation, which "is the means to satisfy man with the righteousness that comes from the Redeemer

---

31. POPE JOHN PAUL II, Encyclical Letter *Dives in Misericordia* (November 30, 1980), 1.

himself."[32] The places where this celebration takes place should be appropriately arranged to foster a spirit of recollection.[33]

Since "pardon, freely granted by God, implies in consequence a real change of life, a gradual elimination of evil within, and a renewal in our way of living," the pastoral staff of shrines should support the pilgrims' perseverance in the fruits of the Spirit in every possible way. They should also be especially attentive to make available that expression of the "total gift of the mercy of God" which is the indulgence. Through indulgences, "the repentant sinner receives a remission of the temporal punishment due for the sins already forgiven as regards the fault."[34] In the profound experience of the "communion of saints" that the pilgrim has in the shrine, it will be easier for him to understand "how much each of us can help others—living or dead—to become ever more intimately united with the Father in heaven."[35]

As for the celebration of the Eucharist, it should be kept in mind that it is the center and the heart of the whole life of the shrine, an event of grace which "contains the Church's entire spiritual wealth."[36] For this reason, it is appropriate that the unity that flows from the sacrament of the Eucharist should be manifested in a special way, by gathering together in one celebration the different groups of visitors. In the same way, the Eucharistic presence of the Lord Jesus should be adored not only by individuals, but also by all pilgrim groups, making use of special pious exercises prepared with great care, as in fact happens in many shrines, based on the

---

32. POPE JOHN PAUL II, Encyclical Letter *Redemptor Hominis* (March 4, 1979), 20.

33. For a basic orientation with regard to the catechesis and the celebration of the sacrament of Reconciliation, cf. Pope John Paul II, Post-Synodal Apostolic Exhortation *Reconciliatio et Paenitentia* (December 2, 1984).

34. POPE JOHN PAUL II, *Bull of Indiction of the Great Jubilee of the Year 2000 Incarnationis Mysterium* (November 20, 1998), 9.

35. *Ibid.,* 10. Cf. POPE PAUL VI, Apostolic Constitution *Indulgentiarum Doctrina* (January 1, 1967).

36. SECOND VATICAN ECUMENICAL COUNCIL, Decree *Presbyterorum Ordinis,* 5.

conviction that the "Eucharist contains and expresses all the forms of prayer."[37]

Above all, the celebration of the sacraments of Reconciliation and the Eucharist gives shrines a particular dignity: "Shrines should not be considered marginal or less important, but rather essential places, places where people go to obtain Grace, even before they obtain graces."[38]

12. A Place of Ecclesial Communion

Given new birth by the Word and the sacraments, those who have come to the shrine of "dead stones" become a shrine of "living stones" and are thus capable of having a *renewed experience* of that communion in faith and holiness that is the Church. In this sense, we can say that a shrine is the place where the Church of people alive in the living God can be reborn. There, each individual can rediscover the gift that the creativity of the Spirit has given to him or her for the benefit of all. In the shrine too, everyone can discern and develop his or her own vocation and become open to living it out in service to others, especially in the parish community, where human differences come together and are articulated in *ecclesial communion*.[39] For this reason, careful attention should be paid to the pastoral care of vocations and of the family, itself the "privileged place and shrine where the great and intimate events in the history of each unique human being are lived out."[40]

Communion with the Holy Spirit, brought about through communion with the sacred realities of the Word and the sacraments,

---

37. *Catechism of the Catholic Church,* 2653; cf. POPE PAUL VI, Encyclical Letter *Mysterium Fidei* (September 3, 1965); CONGREGATION FOR DIVINE WORSHIP, Instruction *Inaestimabile Donum* (April 3, 1980).

38. POPE JOHN PAUL II, *Letter to Archbishop Pasquale Macchi on the Seventh Centenary of the Shrine of the Holy House of Loreto* (August 15, 1993), 7.

39. Cf. SECOND VATICAN ECUMENICAL COUNCIL, Decree *Apostolicam Actuositatem,* 10.

40. POPE JOHN PAUL II, *Address at the General Audience* (January 3, 1979); cf. SECOND VATICAN ECUMENICAL COUNCIL, Decree *Apostolicam Actuositatem,* 11.

gives birth to the communion of saints, God's People, made such by the Holy Spirit. In a particular way, the Virgin Mary, "model of the Church in the order of faith, charity and perfect union with Christ,"[41] venerated in so many shrines,[42] helps the faithful to understand and accept the working of the Holy Spirit that brings about the communion of saints in Christ.

The intense experience of the Church's unity which shrines provide can also help pilgrims to discern and welcome the promptings of the Spirit that lead them in a special way to pray and work for the unity of all Christians.[43] Shrines can be places where ecumenical commitment is strongly promoted, since there the change of heart and holiness of life that are "the soul of the whole ecumenical movement"[44] is fostered and the grace of unity given by the Lord is experienced. In the shrine too, a practical "sharing in spiritual activities and resources" can occur, especially through common prayer and in use of sacred places,[45] which greatly promotes the path of unity when the criteria laid down by Church authorities are fully respected.

This experience of Church must be particularly fostered through the fitting welcome given to pilgrims to the shrine. This should take into consideration the specific characteristics of each group and each individual, the yearnings of their hearts and their authentic spiritual needs.

---

41. SECOND VATICAN ECUMENICAL COUNCIL, Dogmatic Constitution *Lumen Gentium,* 63.

42. As Pope John Paul II has stated: "Marian shrines are like the house of the Mother, refreshment and rest points on the long road that leads to Christ. They are forges, where, through the simple and humble faith of the 'poor in spirit' (cf. Mt 5:3), one comes in contact again with the great wealth that Christ has entrusted and granted to the Church, particularly the sacraments, grace, mercy, charity toward our brothers who are suffering and sick" (*Angelus,* June 21, 1987).

43. Cf. SECOND VATICAN ECUMENICAL COUNCIL, Decree *Unitatis Redintegratio,* 4.

44. *Ibid.,* 8.

45. PONTIFICAL COUNCIL FOR PROMOTING CHRISTIAN UNITY, *Directory for the Application of Principles and Norms on Ecumenism* (March 25, 1993), 29, 103.

In the shrine, we learn to open our heart to everyone, in particular to those who are different from us: the guest, the stranger, the immigrant, the refugee, those of other religions, non-believers. In this way the shrine does not only exist as the setting for an experience of Church, but also becomes a gathering place open to all humanity.

Indeed, it should be realized that on numerous occasions, due to historical and cultural traditions and to greater ease of travel, the Christian faithful are joined in their pilgrimages to shrines both by members of other Churches and ecclesial communities and by the followers of other religions. A certainty that the plan of salvation embraces them too,[46] a recognition of their oftentimes exemplary fidelity to their own religious convictions,[47] and a common experience of the same historical events open new horizons and show the urgency of ecumenical and interreligious dialogue. Shrines can enable this to be carried on in the presence of the holy Mystery of God, who welcomes everyone.[48] At the same time, it must be kept in mind that shrines are meeting places for an encounter with Christ through the Word and the sacraments. Consequently there is need for constant vigilance against all possible forms of syncretism. Shrines are likewise meant to be a sign of contradiction with regard to pseudo-spiritualistic movements, such as the New Age movement. Rather than a generic religious sentiment based exclusively on the heightened use of natural human faculties, shrines strongly insist on the primacy of God and the need to be open to his saving work in Christ for true human fulfillment.

---

46. Cf. Second Vatican Ecumenical Council, Dogmatic Constitution *Lumen Gentium,* 16.

47. Cf. Pope John Paul II, Encyclical Letter *Redemptor Hominis* (March 4, 1979), 6.

48. Cf. Pope John Paul II, Apostolic Letter *Tertio Millennio Adveniente* (November 10, 1994), 52–53.

III. The Shrine, a Prophecy of the Heavenly Homeland

13. A Sign of Hope

The shrine, as a *memory* of our origin in the Lord and a sign of the divine presence, is also a *prophecy* of our ultimate and definitive homeland: the kingdom of God, which will come about when, according to his promise: "I shall set my shrine in their midst forever" (Ez 37:26).

As a sign, the shrine does not only remind us whence we come and who we are, but also opens our eyes to discern where we are going, the goal of our pilgrimage in life and history. The shrine, a work of human hands, points beyond itself to the heavenly Jerusalem, our Mother, the city coming down from God, all adorned as a bride (cf. Rev 21:2), the perfect eschatological shrine where the glorious divine presence is directly and personally experienced: "I could not see any temple in the city, for the Lord Almighty and the Lamb were themselves the temple" (Rev 21:22). In that city and temple there will be no more tears, no more sadness or suffering or death (cf. Rev 21:4).

The shrine thus appears as a *prophetic sign of hope,* an appeal to a broader horizon which discloses the promise that does not disappoint. Amid life's difficulties, the shrine, an edifice of stone, points to the homeland glimpsed from afar but not yet attained, anticipation of which, in faith and hope, sustains Christ's disciples on their pilgrim way. It is significant that after the great trials of the Exile, the Chosen People felt the need to express a sign of their hope by rebuilding the Temple, the shrine of adoration and praise. Israel made every possible sacrifice to restore this sign to her eyes and heart, not only because it would remind her of the love of God who chose her and lived in her midst, but also because it would evoke a yearning for the ultimate goal of the promise toward which God's pilgrims travel in every age. The eschatological event on which the faith of Christians is founded is the rebuilding of the Temple which is the body of the Crucified One, brought about by his glorious resurrection, the pledge of our hope (cf. 1 Cor 15:12–28).

A living icon of this hope is first and foremost the presence in shrines of the sick and the suffering.[49] Meditation on God's saving work helps them understand that through their sufferings they are sharing in a privileged way in the healing power of the redemption accomplished by Christ[50] and proclaiming before the world the victory of the Risen One. Together with them, all those who accompany and assist them with active charity are witnesses of the hope of the kingdom inaugurated by the Lord Jesus, starting precisely with the poor and the suffering: "Go back and tell John what you have seen and heard: the blind see again, the lame walk, lepers are cleansed and the deaf hear, the dead are raised to life, the good news is proclaimed to the poor" (Lk 7:22).

14. An Invitation to Joy

The hope that does not disappoint (cf. Rom 5:5) fills our hearts with joy (cf. Rom 15:13). In shrines, the People of God learns to be the "Church of joy." All who have entered the mystery of the shrine know that God is already at work in our human world which even now, despite the darkness of the present time, is the dawn of the time to come, that the kingdom of God is even now present among us and so our hearts can already be full of joy, trust and hope, in spite of the pain, death, tears and blood that cover the face of the earth.

Psalm 122, one of the psalms sung by the pilgrims journeying toward the Temple, says: "I rejoiced that they said to me, 'Let us go

---

49. Cf. Pope John Paul II, *Homily* at the Mass for the Sick in St. Peter's Basilica (February 11, 1990).

50. Cf. Second Vatican Ecumenical Council, Dogmatic Constitution *Lumen Gentium*, 41; cf. Pope John Paul II, Apostolic Letter *Salvifici Doloris* (February 11, 1984).

to the house of the Lord.'" This witness echoes the sentiments of all those who go to shrines, and above all the joy of meeting their brothers and sisters (cf. Ps 133:1).

In shrines, we celebrate the "joy of forgiveness" that impels us to "celebrate and rejoice" (Lk 15:32), since "there is rejoicing among the angels of God over even a single repentant sinner" (Lk 15:10). There, gathered around the one table of the Word and the Eucharist, we experience the "joy of communion" with Christ that Zaccheus experienced when he welcomed the Lord into his home "with joy" (Lk 19:6). This indeed is the "perfect joy" (Jn 15:11) that no one can ever take away (cf. Jn 16:23), treasured in a faithful heart which has itself become a living temple of the Eternal One, a shrine of flesh for the worship of God in spirit and truth. Together with the Psalmist, each pilgrim is invited to say: "I shall go to the altar of God, to the God of my joy. I will rejoice and praise you on the harp, O God, my God" (Ps 43:4).

15. A Call to Conversion and Renewal

As a sign, the shrine gives witness that we are not made to live and die, but to live and triumph over death through the victory of Christ. As a consequence, the community celebrating its God in the shrine remembers that it is a pilgrim Church journeying toward the Promised Land in a state of *constant conversion and renewal.* The shrine at hand is not the last step of the journey. Tasting the love of God there, the faithful realize that they have not reached their final destination. Instead they sense a more powerful yearning for the heavenly Jerusalem, the desire for heaven. Thus, shrines make us acknowledge both the holiness of those to whom they are dedicated and our condition as sinners who need to begin anew each day the pilgrimage toward God's grace. They make us realize that the Church "is at once holy and ever in need of being purified,"[51] since its members are sinners.

The Word of God helps us to keep this tension alive, especially in the prophetic criticism of shrines which have become places of empty ritual: "Who has asked you to trample through my courts?

---

51. Second Vatican Ecumenical Council, Dogmatic Constitution *Lumen Gentium,* 8; cf. Decree *Unitatis Redintegratio,* 6–7.

Bring no more futile cereal offerings; the smoke from them fills me with disgust. New moons, Sabbaths, assemblies—I cannot endure solemnity combined with guilt.... Cease doing evil. Learn to do good, search for justice, discipline the violent, be just to the orphan, plead for the widow" (Is 1:12–17). Sacrifice pleasing to God is a broken, contrite heart (cf. Ps 51:17). As Jesus affirmed: "It is not anyone who says to me, 'Lord, Lord' who will enter the kingdom of heaven, but the person who does the will of my Father in heaven" (Mt 7:21).

The need for continuous conversion is inseparable from the proclamation of the goal to which theological hope is directed. Every time the community of the faithful gathers together in the shrine, it does so to remind itself of that other shrine, the future city, the dwelling of God, which we wish to begin building already in this world and which we cannot help but desire, filled with hope, conscious of our limitations, striving to prepare as best we can the coming of the kingdom. The mystery of the shrine thus reminds the pilgrim Church on earth of her contingency, of the fact that she is directed to a greater goal, the future homeland, that fills the heart with hope and peace. This stimulus to constant conversion in hope, this witness of the primacy of God's kingdom, of which the Church is the beginning and the first fruits, must be particularly encouraged in the pastoral care which is provided in the shrine, for the growth of the community and of individual believers.

16. A Symbol of the New Heavens and the New Earth

The shrine takes on a *prophetic significance,* because it is a sign of that greater hope that points to the final and definitive destination, where each individual will be fully human, respected and fulfilled according to the righteousness of God. For this reason, the shrine becomes a constant call to critique the myopia of all human projects that would impose themselves as absolutes. It can therefore be considered a protest against every worldly presumption, against every political dictatorship, against every ideology that claims to say everything there is to be said about man, since it reminds us that there is another dimension, the kingdom of God, that is yet to come in its fullness. In the shrine, the *Magnificat* is constantly echoed. There the Church "sees uprooted that sin which is found at the early history of man and woman, the sin of disbelief and of 'little faith' in God"; there, "Mary boldly proclaims the undimmed truth about God: the holy and almighty God, who from the beginning is the source of all gifts, he who 'has done great things in her.'"[52]

Shrines bear witness to the eschatological dimension of the Christian faith, the tension experienced as it moves toward the fullness of the kingdom. This is the foundation and source of the moral and political vocation of the faithful to offer, in history, a critical reading of human projects in the light of the Gospel, one that reminds men and women of their higher destiny, prevents them from being impoverished by the myopia of materialism and obliges them to serve unceasingly as the leaven (cf. Mt 13:33) of a more just and more humane society.

Precisely because they are reminders of another dimension, that of the "new heavens and the new earth" (Rev 21:1), shrines stimulate us to live as a critical and prophetic ferment in these present heavens and in this present earth and they renew the vocation of Christians to live in the world, while not being of the world (cf. Jn 17:16). This vocation is a rejection of the ideological exploitation of any sign whatsoever, in order to be a stimulating presence at the service of the edification of the whole person in each person, according to the will of the Lord.

In this light, we can understand how a thoughtful plan of pastoral action can make shrines places of education in ethical values, particularly justice, solidarity, peace and the protection of creation, and thus contribute to the growth of quality of life for everyone.

---

52. Pope John Paul II, Encyclical Letter *Redemptoris Mater* (March 25, 1987), 37.

Conclusion

17. A Convergence of Efforts

Shrines are not only human achievements, but also visible signs of the presence of the invisible God. For this reason, they call for an appropriate *convergence of human efforts* and a proper awareness of the roles and responsibilities of those concerned with the pastoral care which they provide, precisely to bring about a full recognition and a fruitful reception of the gift that the Lord gives to his people through each shrine.

Shrines offer a valuable service to the individual particular Churches, above all by making available the proclamation of the Word of God and the celebration of the sacraments of Reconciliation and the Eucharist.[53] This service expresses and strengthens the historical and spiritual bonds linking shrines with the Churches in whose heart they were born. It demands that the pastoral action carried out by the shrine should be fully incorporated into that of the bishops, with particular concern for what pertains particularly to the "charism" of the place and the spiritual benefit of the faithful who go there on pilgrimage.

Under the guidance of the individual bishops or of the whole episcopal conference, depending on each case, the specific pastoral identity and organizational structure of shrines should be defined

---

53. On the other hand, it is particularly appropriate that the sacraments of Baptism, Confirmation and Matrimony be celebrated in the parish of residence; in this way the faithful will be helped to grasp the community significance of these sacraments; cf. POPE JOHN PAUL II, Apostolic Exhortation *Christifideles Laici* (December 30, 1988), 26.

in their proper statutes.[54] The sharing of shrines in the diocesan plan of pastoral care requires that arrangements be made for the specific preparation of the persons and the communities to which each shrine is entrusted.

It is equally important for cooperation and forms of association between shrines to be encouraged, especially among those in the same geographical and cultural area, as well as the coordination of their pastoral activity with the pastoral care of tourists and human mobility in general. The remarkable growth of such initiatives—from international congresses to continental and national meetings[55]—calls attention to the increasing numbers of people visiting shrines. It is also a reminder of pressing new needs and has given rise to new pastoral responses to the changing challenges of places and time.

The "mystery of the temple" thus offers a wealth of possibilities for meditation and fruitful activity. As a *memory* of our origin, the shrine calls to mind God's initiative and helps pilgrims to recognize it with a sense of awe, gratitude and commitment. As a place of the divine *presence,* it bear witness to God's faithfulness and his constant activity in the midst of his people, through his Word and the sacraments. As a *prophecy,* or a reminder of our heavenly homeland, it makes us remember that everything is not finished, but must yet be accomplished fully in accordance with God's promise which is our goal. Precisely by showing the relativity of everything penultimate in regard to our ultimate homeland, shrines point to Christ as the new Temple of mankind reconciled with God.

Keeping in mind these three theological dimensions of the shrine, the pastoral care provided in shrines should be concerned to foster a constant renewal of the spiritual life and of commitment to the Church, in an intense and critical vigilance toward all cultures and

---

54. *Code of Canon Law,* can. 1232. The French Episcopal Conference, for example, has issued a *Charter of Shrines.*

55. The Pontifical Council for the Pastoral Care of Migrants and Itinerant People is active in this area, as is demonstrated by its organization of two World Congresses (Rome, February 26–29, 1992, and Ephesus, Turkey, May 4–7, 1998) and two at a regional level (Máriapocs, Hungary, September 2–4, 1996 and Pompeii, Italy, October 17–21, 1998), cf. the relative Proceedings.

human achievements, yet also in a spirit of cooperation, open to the demands of ecumenical and interreligious dialogue.

18. Mary, the Living Shrine

The Virgin Mary is the living shrine of the Word of God, the Ark of the New and Eternal Covenant. In fact, St. Luke's account of the annunciation of the angel to Mary nicely incorporates the images of the tent of meeting with God in Sinai and of the Temple of Zion. Just as the cloud covered the people of God marching in the desert (cf. Nm 10:34; Dt 33:12; Ps 91:4) and just as the same cloud, as a sign of the divine mystery present in the midst of Israel, hovered over the Ark of the Covenant (cf. Ex 40:35), so now the shadow of the Most High envelops and penetrates the tabernacle of the new covenant that is the womb of Mary (cf. Lk 1:35).

Indeed, Luke the evangelist subtly links the words of the angel to the song that the prophet Zephaniah raises to the presence of God in Zion. To Mary, the angel says: "Rejoice, you who are filled with God's grace! The Lord is with you.... Mary, do not be afraid.... You are to conceive in your womb and bear a son..." (Lk 1:28–31). To Zion, the prophet says: "Rejoice, exult with all your heart, daughter of Jerusalem!... The Lord is king among you, Israel, you have nothing more to fear.... Zion, have no fear...the Lord your God is there with you, the warrior-Savior" (Zeph 3:14–17). In the "womb" *(be qereb)* of the daughter of Zion, symbol of Jerusalem, site of the Temple, the presence of God with his people is made manifest. In the womb of the new daughter of Zion, the Lord establishes his perfect temple in order to have full communion with mankind through his Son, Jesus Christ.

This theme is reasserted in the scene of Mary's visit to Elizabeth. The question that the latter addresses to the future mother of Jesus is significant: "Why should I be honored with a visit from the mother of my Lord?" (Lk 1:43). Her words evoke those of David before the Ark of the Lord: "How can the ark of Yahweh come to be with me?" (2 Sam 6:9). Mary is thus the new Ark of the Lord's presence. In passing we may note that here the title *Kyrios,* "Lord," applied to Christ, appears for the first time in the Gospel of Luke. This is the title that translated the sacred name *YHWH* in the Greek Bible. Just as the ark of the Lord remained in the house of Obed-Edom for three months, filling it with blessings (cf. 2 Sam 6:11), so too Mary, the living Ark of God, remained three months in the house of Elizabeth with her sanctifying presence (cf. Lk 1:56).

Here the statement of St. Ambrose is instructive: "Mary was the temple of God, not the God of the temple; hence only he who was at work in the temple is to be adored."[56] For this reason, "the Church, throughout her life, maintains with the Mother of God a link which embraces, in the saving mystery, the *past,* the *present* and the *future,* and venerates her as the spiritual mother of humanity and the advocate of grace,"[57] as is shown by the presence of numerous Marian shrines all over the world,[58] which constitute an authentic "missionary Magnificat."[59]

In the many Marian shrines, the Holy Father states, "not only individuals or local groups, but sometimes whole nations and societies, even whole continents, seek to meet the Mother of the Lord, the one who is blessed because she believed, is the first among believers and therefore became the Mother of Emmanuel. This is the message of the Land of Palestine, the spiritual homeland of all Christians because it was the homeland of the Savior of the world and of his Mother. This is the message of the many churches in Rome and throughout the world which have been raised up in the course of the centuries by the faith of Christians. This is the message of centers like Guadalupe, Lourdes, Fatima and the others situated in the various countries. Among them how could I fail to mention the one in my own native land, Jasna Gora?

---

56. *De Spiritu Sancto,* III, 11:80.

57. POPE JOHN PAUL II, Encyclical Letter *Redemptoris Mater* (March 25, 1987), 47.

58. POPE JOHN PAUL II reminds us: "I know very well that every people, every country, indeed every diocese, has its holy places in which the heart of the whole People of God beats, one could say, in more lively fashion: places of special encounter between God and human beings; places in which Christ dwells in a special way in our midst. If these places are so often dedicated to his Mother, it reveals all the more fully to us the nature of his Church," *Homily* at the Shrine of Our Lady of Knock, Ireland (September 30, 1979).

59. POPE JOHN PAUL II, Message to the Third Latin American Missionary Congress (Bogotá, July 6, 1987).

One could perhaps speak of a specific 'geography' of faith and Marian devotion, which includes all these special places of pilgrimage where the People of God seek to meet the Mother of God in order to find, within the radius of the maternal presence of her 'who believed,' a strengthening of their own faith."[60]

To this end, those who are responsible for the pastoral care of shrines should be ever attentive that the various expressions of Marian piety are integrated into the liturgical life which is the center and the very meaning of the shrine.

In approaching Mary, pilgrims should feel themselves called to experience that "paschal dimension"[61] which gradually transforms their life through the hearing of the Word, the celebration of the sacraments and a commitment on behalf of their brothers and sisters.

From the encounter of communities and individuals with Mary, "Star of evangelization,"[62] pilgrims, like the apostles before them, will be impelled to proclaim by word and by witness of life "the mighty works of God" (Acts 2:11).

Vatican City, May 8, 1999.

ARCHBISHOP STEPHEN FUMIO HAMAO
President

ARCHBISHOP FRANCESCO GIOIA
Secretary

---

60. POPE JOHN PAUL II, Encyclical Letter *Redemptoris Mater* (March 25, 1987), 28.

61. CONGREGATION FOR DIVINE WORSHIP, Circular Letter to the Presidents of the National Liturgical Commissions *Orientamenti e proposte per la celebrazione dell'Anno mariano* (April 3, 1987), 78. *Notitiae* 23 (1987), p. 386.

62. POPE PAUL VI, Apostolic Exhortation *Evangelii Nuntiandi* (December 8, 1975), 82.

Bibliography

General

Alimenti, Dante. *Lourdes, Fatima, Guadalupe: Les Apparitions de la Vierge*. Italy: Editrice Velar, 1988.

Aston, Joan. *Mother of All Nations: The Visitations of the Blessed Virgin and Her Message for Today*. San Francisco: Harper & Row, 1989.

Bartholomew, Courtenay. *A Scientist Researches Mary: The Ark of the Covenant*. Asbury, New Jersey: 101 Foundation, 1996.

Brown, Michael. *The Final Hour*. Milford, Ohio: Faith Publishing, 1992.

Brown, Raphael. *Saints Who Saw Mary*. Rockford, Illinois: Tan Books and Publishers, 1994.

Cruz, Joan Carroll. *The Incorruptibles*. Rockford, Illinois: Tan Books and Publishers, 1977.

————. *Miraculous Images of Our Lady*. Rockford, Illinois: Tan Books and Publishers, 1993.

Durham, Michael. *Miracles of Mary: Apparitions, Legends and Miraculous Works of the Blessed Virgin Mary*. San Francisco: Harper, 1995.

Flinders, Carol Less. *Enduring Grace: Living Portraits of Seven Women Mystics*. San Francisco: Harper, 1993.

Flynn, Ted and Maureen. *The Thunder of Justice*. Sterling, Virginia: Max Kol Communications, 1993.

Freeze, Michael. *Voices, Visions and Apparitions*. Huntington, Indiana: Our Sunday Visitor, 1993.

Groeschel, Benedict J. *A Still, Small, Voice: A Practical Guide on Reported Revelations*. San Francisco: Ignatius Press, 1993.

Hebert, Albert. *Mary, Why Do You Cry?* Paulina, Louisiana: 1985.

Higgins, Paul Lambourne. *Pilgrimages: A Guide to the Holy Places of Europe for Today's Traveler*. Englewood Cliffs, New Jersey: Prentice-Hall, 1984.

Hoagland, Victor. *The Book of Saints*. Farmingdale, New York: Regina Press, 1986.

Laurentin, René. *The Apparitions of the Blessed Virgin Mary Today*. Dublin: Veritas Publications, 1991.

Le Blanc, Sr. Mary Francis. *Cause of Our Joy*. Boston: Pauline Books & Media, 1976, 1991.

Lord, Bob and Penny. *The Many Faces of Mary: A Love Story*. Westlake Village, California: Journeys of Faith, 1987.

Marucci, Domenico. *Sanctuari Mariani d'Italia*. Milano: Edizioni Paoline, 1987.

———. *Sanctuari Mariani d'Europa*. Milano: Edizioni Paoline, 1993.

McNaspy, C. J. *A Guide to Christian Europe*. Chicago: Loyola University Press, 1984.

McClure, Kevin. *The Evidence for Visions of the Virgin Mary*. England: Thorsons Publishers, 1984.

Nolan, Mary Lee and Sidney Nolan. *Christian Pilgrimage in Modern Western Europe*. Chapel Hill: University of North Carolina Press, 1989.

O'Carroll, Michael. *Theotokos: A Theological Encyclopedia of the Blessed Virgin Mary*. Collegeville, Minnesota: The Liturgical Press, 1982.

Odell, Catherine M. *Those Who Saw Her: The Apparitions of Mary*. Huntington, Indiana: Our Sunday Visitor, 1986.

Pichette, Daniel. *La Vierge inconnue*. Quebec: Multicopie Estrie, 1990.

Rosage, David. *Mary, Star of the New Millennium*. Ann Arbor, Michigan: Servant Publications, 1997.

Saggiorato, Benvenuto Angelo. *La Madonna nel mondo*. Padova: Edizioni Caroccio, 1986.

Seward, Desmond. *The Dancing Sun: Journeys to the Miraculous Shrines*. London: Flaunt, 1993.

Sherry, Gerard. *The Catholic Shrines of Europe*. Huntington, Indiana: Our Sunday Visitor, 1986.

Sharkey, Don. *The Woman Shall Conquer*. Libertyville, Illinois: Prow Books, 1954.

Zimdars-Swartz, Sandra L. *Encountering Mary: From La Salette to Medjugorje*. Princeton: Princeton University Press, 1991.

Akita, Japan

Fujita, Neil. *Japan's Encounter with Christianity*. Mahwah, New Jersey: Paulist Press, 1991.

Fukushima, Francis Mutsuo. *Akita: Mother of God as Co-Redemptrix*. Santa Barbara: Queenship, 1994.

Haffert, John M. *The Meaning of Akita*. Asbury, New Jersey: 101 Foundation, 1990.

Harrington, Ann. *Japan's Hidden Christians*. Chicago: Loyola University Press, 1993.

Jacq, Joseph-Marie. *Celle qui pleure au Japon*. Paris: Tequi, 1985.

Yasuda, Teiji. *Akita: The Tears and Message of Mary*. Asbury, New Jersey: 101 Foundation, 1990.

Banneux, Belgium

Abbaye du Mont-Cesar. *Banneux Notre Dame*. Louvain: Editions du Mont-César, 1950.

Les huit apparitions de Banneux Notre Dame. Banneux: Secretariat.

Ruffle, Sheila. *Banneux: The Virgin of the Poor—The Story of the Apparitions*. Liege: Bel Art S.A., 1979.

Wuillaume, L. *Banneux: Message pour notre temps*. Banneux: les Sanctuaires de Banneux, 1983.

Beauraing, Belgium

Charue, Yves M. *Beauraing: Our Lady of the Heart of Gold.* Translated by Edmund Dougan, OFM. Beauraing: Editions Pro Maria, 1991.

Poisson, Doris. *The Apparitions of Our Lady at Beauraing.* Lowell, Massachusetts: Pro Maria Committee.

Toussaint, F. and C. Joset. *Beauraing: Les apparitions.* France: L'imprimerie Saint-Paul, 1981.

Betania, Venezuela

Aristizabal, Father Otty Ossa. *Apariciones de la Virgen Maria en Betania.* Caracas: San Pablo, 1993.

Brown, M. *The Bridge to Heaven.* Lima, Pennsylvania: Marian Communications Ltd., 1993.

Eck, Larry and Mary Sue. "Land of Grace." *Medjugorje Magazine,* January–March, 68–71.

Karminski, Stanley. "Bishop Approves Apparitions in Venezuela." *Queen,* May–June 1990, 4–8.

Pio Bello Ricardo. *Instruccion pastoral sobre las apariciones de la santisima Virgen en finca Betania.* Los Teques, 1987.

Sims, Sister Margaret Catherine. *Apparitions in Betania, Venezuela.* Framingham, Massachusetts: Medjugorje Messengers, 1992.

Fatima, Portugal

Albani, Angelo and Massimo Astrua. *Storia illustrata di Fatima.* Vicenza, Italy: Edizioni Istituto S. Gaetano, 1985.

Alonso, Joaquim Maria and Abilo Pina Ribeiro. *Fatima: Message and Consecration.* Fatima: Consolata Missions' Publications, 1984.

Baker, G. Leslie. *The Finger of God Is Here.* Ireland: St. Paul Publications, 1961.

Cappa, Alphonse. *Fatima: Cove of Wonders.* Boston: Pauline Books & Media, 1979.

De Marchi, John. *Fatima from the Beginning*. 8th ed. Fatima: Missoes Consolata, 1991.

Fox, Robert. *Rediscovering Fatima*. Huntington, Indiana: Our Sunday Visitor, 1982.

Galamba de Oliveira, Rev. Joseph. *Jacinta: The Flower of Fatima*. Washington, New Jersey: AMI Press, 1982.

Hebert, Albert. *The Tears of Mary and Fatima*. Paulina, Louisiana, 1993.

Kondor, Louis, ed. *Fatima in Lucia's Own Words*. Fatima: Postulation Center, 1989.

Pelletier, Joseph. *The Sun Danced at Fatima*. New York: Image, 1983.

Rengers, Christopher. *The Youngest Prophet: The Life of Jacinta Marto*. New York: Alba House, 1986.

Rossi, Severo and Aventino de Oliveiro. *Fatima*. Fatima: Consolata Mission's Publications, 1981.

Walsh, William Thomas. *Our Lady of Fatima*. 3rd ed. New York: Image, 1990.

Guadalupe, Mexico

Carroll, Warren H. *Our Lady of Guadalupe and the Conquest of Darkness*. Front Royal, Virginia: Christendom Publications, 1983.

Dooley, L. M. *That Motherly Mother of Guadalupe*. Boston: Pauline Books & Media, 1979.

Eliot, Ethel Cook. "Our Lady of Guadalupe in Mexico." In *A Woman Clothed with the Sun: Eight Great Appearances of Our Lady*. New York: Image, 1961.

Elizondo, Virgil. *Guadalupe: Mother of the New Creation*. Maryknoll, NY: Orbis Books, 1997.

Feeney, Robert. *Mother of the Americas*. Forest Grove, Oregon: Aquinas Press, 1983.

Franciscan Friars of the Immaculate. *A Handbook on Guadalupe*. Waite Parke, Minnesota: Park Press, 1996.

Johnston, Francis. *The Wonder of Guadalupe*. Rockford, Illinois: Tan Books and Publishers, 1981.

Rengers, Christopher. *Mary of the Americas: Our Lady of Guadalupe*. New York: Alba House, 1989.

Knock, Ireland

Coyne, William D. *Venerable Archdeacon Cavanagh: Pastor of Knock (1867–1897)*. Knock: Knock Shrine Society, 1990.

Hubert, Father. *Knock: Vision of Hope*. Knock: Knock Shrine Society, 1989.

Neary, Tom. *I Comforted Them in Sorrow, Knock: 1879–1979*. Knock: The Custodians of Knock Shrine, 1979.

———. *I Saw Our Lady*. Knock: The Custodians of Knock Shrine, 1989.

Our Lady's Shrine: A Pilgrim's Guide Book. Knock: Knock Shrine Society, 1980.

Purcell, Mary. "Our Lady of Silence." In *A Woman Clothed with the Sun: Eight Great Appearances of Our Lady*. New York: Image, 1961.

Walsh, Berchmans. *Knock: Mary's International Shrine of the Lamb of God*. Knock: Knock Shrine Society, 1985.

Krakow, Poland

Kosicki, George W. *Now Is the Time for Mercy*. Stockbridge, Massachusetts: Marian Press, 1993.

Kowalska, Sister M. Faustina. *Divine Mercy in My Soul: The Diary of Sister Faustina*. Stockbridge, Massachusetts: Marian Press, 1987.

Michalenko, Sister Sophia. *Mercy Is My Mission: The Life of Sister Faustina H. Kowalska*. Stockbridge, Massachusetts: Marian Press, 1987.

Michalenko, Fr. Seraphim and Vinny Flynn. *The Divine Mercy Message and Devotion*. Stockbridge, Massachusetts: Marian Press, 1993.

Tarnawska, Maria. *Sister Faustina Kowalska: Her Life and Mission*. Stockbridge, Massachusetts: Marian Press, 1989.

La Salette, France

Castel, Roger and Marjorie Cox. *Our Lady of La Salette*. Corps.

Flachot, Andre. *La Salette du Haut-Vaugirard*. Paris: Editions Fondation le Prevost, 1985.

Gouin, Abbe. *Sister Mary of the Cross: Shepherdess of La Salette*. London: Billings, 1981.

Lourdes, France

Astrua, Massino. *Storia illustrata di Lourdes*. Vicenza, Italy: Edizioni Istituto S. Gaetano, 1970.

Ausina, Gerard and Luigi Prodomi. *Lourdes: La ciudad Marial en color*. Lourdes: Editions Andre Doucet, 1991.

Bordes, Joseph. *Lourdes in Bernadette's Footsteps*. Vic-en-Bigorre, France: MSM, 1991.

Bernardo, Antonio. *Past and Present Lourdes*. Lourdes: Etablissements Estrade, 1991.

Caujolle, Marie. *Lourdes: From Vision to Pilgrimage*. Vic-en-Bigorre, France, MSM: 1994.

Costi, Pio. *Lourdes: City of Our Lady*. Firenze, Italy: Casa Editrice Bonechi, 1979.

Cranston, Ruth. *The Miracle of Lourdes*. New York: Image, 1988.

Laurentin, René. *Bernadette vous parle*. Paris, France: Apostolat des Editions, 1972.

Lourdes: The Wondrous Story of Bernadette Soubirous. Bologna: Editions Halcards.

Lynch, John W. *Bernadette: The Only Witness*. Boston: Pauline Books & Media, 1981.

Trochu, Francois. *St. Bernadette Soubirous*. Rockford, Illinois: Tan Books and Publishers, 1985.

Paray-le-Monial, France

Bougaud, Emile. *The Life of St. Margaret Mary Alacoque*. Rockford, Illinois: Tan Books and Publishers, 1990.

Croiset, John. *The Devotion to the Sacred Heart of Jesus*. Rockford, Illinois: Tan Books and Publishers, 1988.

Ladame, Jean. *St. Margaret Mary and the Visitation in Paray*. Lyons: Editions Résiac, 1994.

Monastère de la Visitation. Discover the Heart of Jesus with Margaret Mary in Paray-le-Monial. Paris: Jet Realisations, 1998.

Richomme, Agnes. *Marguerite-Marie: L'Amour du coeur de Jesus*. France: L'imprimerie de Montligeon, 1996.

The Autobiography of St. Margaret Mary Alacoque. Rockford, Illinois: Tan Books and Publishers, 1986.

Cristiani, Leon. *St. Margaret Mary Alacoque and the Promises of the Sacred Heart*. Boston: Pauline Books & Media, 1975.

Pontmain, France

Badiche, Anne-Marie. *Pontmain*. France: Editions Ouest-France, 1990.

Bessieres, Helene. *La prophetie de Notre Dame a Pontmain*. Montsurs: Editions Résiac, 1988.

Laurentin, René. *The Apparition at Pontmain*. Laval: L'imprimerie R. Madiot, 1987.

———— and A. Durand. *Pontmain: Histoire authentique*. Un signe dans le ciel. 4th ed. Laval, France: R. Madiot, 1990.

Richard, M., and J. Haffert, trans. *What Happened at Pontmain?* Washington, New Jersey: AMI Press, 1971.

Rue du Bac, Paris

Chierotti, Luigi. *Les apparitions de la medaille miraculeuse*. Montsurs: Editions Résiac, 1988.

Dirvin, Joseph. *St. Catherine Labouré of the Miraculous Medal*. Rockford, Illinois: Tan Books and Publishers, 1984.

Laurentin, René. *Vie de Catherine Labouré*. Bourges: Tardy Quercy, 1990.

Zeitoun, Cairo

Hegomenos Boutross Gayed. *The Apparition of the Virgin Mary at El-Zeitoun Church*. Cairo: St. Mary Coptic Orthodox Church, 1985.

Johnston, Francis. *When Millions Saw Mary*. Devon: Augustine Publishing Company, 1980.

Mansour, Fawzi. *St. Mary's Apparitions at the Coptic Orthodox Church of Zeitoun, Cairo*. Cairo: Printing Office of the French Institute of Oriental Archeology, 1969.

Nil, Michel. *Les Apparitions de la tres Sainte Vierge Marie en Egypte en 1968–1969*. Paris: Tequi, 1980.

Zaki, Pearl. *Our Lord's Mother Visits Egypt in 1968 and 1969*. East Brunswick, New Jersey: St. Mary Coptic Orthodox Church.

BOOKS & MEDIA

The Daughters of St. Paul operate book and media centers at the following addresses. Visit, call or write the one nearest you today, or find us on the World Wide Web, www.pauline.org

CALIFORNIA
3908 Sepulveda Blvd., Culver City, CA 90230   310-397-8676
5945 Balboa Ave., San Diego, CA 92111   858-565-9181
46 Geary Street, San Francisco, CA 94108   415-781-5180

FLORIDA
145 S.W. 107th Ave., Miami, FL 33174   305-559-6715

HAWAII
1143 Bishop Street, Honolulu, HI 96813   808-521-2731
Neighbor Islands call: 800-259-8463

ILLINOIS
172 North Michigan Ave., Chicago, IL 60601   312-346-4228

LOUISIANA
4403 Veterans Memorial Blvd., Metairie, LA 70006   504-887-7631

MASSACHUSETTS
Rte. 1, 885 Providence Hwy., Dedham, MA 02026   781-326-5385

MISSOURI
9804 Watson Rd., St. Louis, MO 63126   314-965-3512

NEW JERSEY
561 U.S. Route 1, Wick Plaza, Edison, NJ 08817   732-572-1200

NEW YORK
150 East 52nd Street, New York, NY 10022   212-754-1110
78 Fort Place, Staten Island, NY 10301   718-447-5071

OHIO
2105 Ontario Street (at Prospect Ave.), Cleveland, OH 44115
216-621-9427

PENNSYLVANIA
9171-A Roosevelt Blvd., Philadelphia, PA 19114   215-676-9494

SOUTH CAROLINA
243 King Street, Charleston, SC 29401   843-577-0175

TENNESSEE
4811 Poplar Ave., Memphis, TN 38117   901-761-2987

TEXAS
114 Main Plaza, San Antonio, TX 78205   210-224-8101

VIRGINIA
1025 King Street, Alexandria, VA 22314   703-549-3806

CANADA
3022 Dufferin Street, Toronto, Ontario, Canada M6B 3T5
416-781-9131
1155 Yonge Street, Toronto, Ontario, Canada M4T 1W2;
416-934-3440

¡También somos su fuente para libros, videos y música en español!